# TOTAL
## OBEDIENCE

Walking Obediently with God In Our Journey On Earth

### Sophia Mitchell

**TOTAL OBEDIENCE**
Walking Obediently with God in Our Journey on Earth.

**Published by:**

**Joy of Many Generations Ltd.**
info@joyofmanygenerations.com
Telephone: +44 (0) 7914 945 246
www.joyofmanygenerations.com

Copyright © 2025 **Sophia Mitchell**
The Copyright Designs and Patent Act 1988 have asserted the author's moral right.

**ISBN: 978-1-0682074-0-2**

All rights reserved. No part of this publication may be reproduced, distributed, or transmitted in any form or by any means, including photocopying, recording, or other electronic or mechanical methods, without prior written permission from the publisher, except in the case of brief quotations embodied in reviews, articles, or other non-commercial uses permitted by copyright law.

This book contains quotations from the following Bible translations, used by permission:

**New King James Version (NKJV)** – Scripture taken from the New King James Version®. Copyright © 1982 by Thomas Nelson. Used by permission. All rights reserved.

**King James Version (KJV)** – Public Domain.

**The Message (MSG)** – Scripture taken from *The Message*. Copyright © 1993, 2002, 2018 by Eugene H. Peterson. Used by permission of NavPress, represented by Tyndale House Publishers, Inc. All rights reserved.

**Amplified Bible (AMP)** – Scripture taken from the Amplified® Bible. Copyright © 2015 by The Lockman Foundation. Used by permission. All rights reserved. www.lockman.org.

**Amplified Bible, Classic Edition (AMPC)** – Scripture quotations taken from the Amplified® Bible, Classic Edition. Copyright © 1954,

1958, 1962, 1964, 1965, 1987 by The Lockman Foundation. Used by permission. All rights reserved. www.lockman.org.

**Christian Standard Bible (CSB)** – Scripture taken from the Christian Standard Bible®. Copyright © 2017 by Holman Bible Publishers. Used by permission. All rights reserved.

**Easy English Bible 2024 (EEB)** – Scripture taken from the Easy English Bible. Copyright © 2024 by MissionAssist. Used by permission. All rights reserved.

**English Standard Version (ESV)** – Scripture quotations taken from the ESV® Bible (The Holy Bible, English Standard Version®), copyright © 2001 by Crossway, a publishing ministry of Good News Publishers. Used by permission. All rights reserved.

**New International Version (NIV)** – Scripture taken from the Holy Bible, New International Version®. NIV®. Copyright © 1973, 1978, 1984, 2011 by Biblica, Inc.™ Used by permission. All rights reserved worldwide.

**New Living Translation (NLT)** – Scripture quotations taken from the Holy Bible, New Living Translation, copyright © 1996, 2004, 2015 by Tyndale House Foundation. Used by permission of Tyndale House Publishers, Inc., Carol Stream, Illinois 60188. All rights reserved.

**World Messianic Bible (WMB)** – Public Domain.

**Legacy Standard Bible (LSB)** – Scripture taken from the Legacy Standard Bible®, copyright © 2021 by The Lockman Foundation. Used by permission. All rights reserved.

Cepher @ 2024 Publishing Group. All rights reserved

**For bulk purchases, speaking engagements and other enquiries, please contact the author at:**
**Email: sophiajamesfunke@gmail.com**
**Phone: +447486428153**
**Printed in the United Kingdom.**

# Table of Contents

ENDORSEMENT ................................................................................ VI

DEDICATION .................................................................................. VII

ACKNOWLEDGEMENTS.................................................................. VIII

FOREWORD ......................................................................................X

PREFACE ...................................................................................... XIII

INTRODUCTION ........................................................................... XIV

**CHAPTER ONE: KNOWING THE TRUE GOD**........................................1

THE ATTRIBUTES OF GOD......................................................................3
*His Faithfulness*................................................................................. 3
ABRAHAM FAITHFULNESS TO GOD..........................................................7
HIS HOLINESS.................................................................................... 11
*Job's confidence in God* ...................................................................15
*His Power*........................................................................................19
*His Words*........................................................................................23
*His Glory* .........................................................................................27
*His Presence*....................................................................................30
GOD'S LOVE FOR US........................................................................... 34
*The Prodigal son*..............................................................................35
*God's amazing grace*........................................................................36
*God's love on the criminal on the cross* ...........................................38

**CHAPTER TWO: TOTAL OBEDIENCE TO GOD** ............................... 41

OUR OBEDIENCE IS WHAT HONOURS GOD ........................................... 43
THE LIGHT SHINES EVEN IN THE DARKEST MOMENTS ........................... 46
OBEDIENCE TO SURRENDER TO HIS WILL............................................. 50
BEYOND WORDS ................................................................................ 52
OUR OBEDIENCE COMPELS HIM TO BE FAITHFUL TOWARDS US ........................ 58
DISOBEDIENCE TO GOD'S COMMANDMENTS IS DANGEROUS............................. 60
HOW TO BE OBEDIENT TO GOD ELOHIYM............................................. 67
PRAYER OF CONFESSION .................................................................... 68

## CHAPTER THREE: UNDERSTANDING YOUR PRIESTHOOD ....... 70

OUR MISSION HERE ON EARTH ................................................................ 72
IT'S ALL ABOUT ELOHIYM ...................................................................... 75
IMAGE OF THE BEAST ............................................................................ 78
TIME TO SURRENDER TO ELOHIYM ......................................................... 83
OFFICE OF THE PRIESTHOOD .................................................................. 88
*Sons and daughters to manifest Him* ................................................... 90
*Qualities we must attain to operate in the office of the priesthood* ... 97
*The office of an intercessor in the priesthood* ................................... 107
GOD'S EXPECTATION ............................................................................ 112
BE FOCUSED ON YOUR ASSIGNMENTS ................................................... 117
PAUL WARNS THE CHURCH .................................................................. 119
THE SCATTERING HORNS ..................................................................... 121
ELI THE PRIEST .................................................................................... 125

## CHAPTER FOUR: KNOWING YOUR TIME OF VISITATION ....... 131

BE WISE AND BE PREPARED ALWAYS .................................................... 134
THE TIME IS CLOSER THAN YOU THINK ................................................. 139
IMPATIENCE DESTROYS GREAT DESTINIES ............................................ 142
ZACCHAEUS' ENCOUNTER WITH JESUS .................................................. 143
GOD DESPISES THE MAN WITH PRIDE ................................................... 144

## CHAPTER FIVE: DIVINE PRESENCE OF GOD ................................. 148

GOD'S INTERVENTION .......................................................................... 149
THE PRESENCE OF ELOHIYM IS OUR SHIELD .......................................... 153
*The benefits of the presence of Elohiym in our lives* ........................ 167

## CHAPTER SIX: HONOUR AND RESPECT ......................................... 172

DIFFERENCE BETWEEN HONOUR AND DISHONOUR ................................ 175
MEN THAT HONOURED ELOHIYM .......................................................... 178
HONOUR TO THE HANDMAIDEN ............................................................ 189
ELOHIYM DESPISES THE PERSON OF PRIDE ........................................... 195
WHO DO WE HONOUR? ........................................................................ 200

## CHAPTER SEVEN: FEARLESS ............................................................ 206

BE BOLD AS A LION ............................................................................. 210
KNOWING THE TRUTH IS WHAT EMPOWERS YOU .................................. 213
FAITH IN THE ALMIGHTY GOD MAKES YOU FEARLESS ......................... 215

FEARLESS DANIEL .................................................................................. 217
DO WE OBEY GOD'S WORD OR MEN'S WORD? ...................................... 221
REASON TO REJOICE ALWAYS ................................................................ 223
UNCOMPROMISING FAITH ...................................................................... 225
ALL POWERS ARE HIS ............................................................................. 229
STUDY TO BE APPROVED BY THE ALMIGHTY GOD ................................. 232

## CHAPTER EIGHT: GOD'S BEST FRIEND .................................. 234

OUR RELATIONSHIP WITH GOD IS SO IMPORTANT ................................ 236
DOING HIS WILL MAKES US HIS FRIEND ............................................... 238
REASON WHY ELOHIYM CALLED ABRAHAM HIS FRIEND ...................... 243
TOTAL COMMITMENT TO GOD IS WHAT MAKES YOU HIS FRIEND ........ 248

## CHAPTER NINE: LIVING A LIFE OF FULFILMENT ................... 252

ONLY WHEN WE ARE CONNECTED TO HIM CAN WE BE FULFILLED ....... 253
HUMAN'S RESPONSIBILITY OVER THE EARTH ....................................... 257
THE REASON PEOPLE PERISH ................................................................. 258
BELIEVE AND ACT ................................................................................... 260
HAVE THE REVELATION OF CHRIST ...................................................... 261
BRINGING GLORY TO HIS NAME ........................................................... 262
WILLING TO FOLLOW HIM TO THE END ............................................... 265
PETER'S REVELATION .............................................................................. 267
THE UNITY OF THE BODY OF YAHUSHA ............................................... 268
A NEW MAN ............................................................................................ 270
YOUR MINDSET SHAPES YOUR DESTINY ............................................... 272
EXTRAORDINARY LIFE IN CHRIST .......................................................... 274
UNHOLY LIFESTYLE CAN STOP US FROM FULFILLING OUR DESTINY .... 276
YOUR DESTINY IS WRITTEN IN A BOOK ................................................ 278

## CHAPTER TEN : EXCEEDING JOY ............................................ 281

THE RESURRECTION OF THE MESSIAH .................................................. 284
HANNAH'S JOY ....................................................................................... 286
HANNAH'S PRAYER ................................................................................. 286
THE CHOSEN ONES ................................................................................ 287
PRAYER .................................................................................................... 289

## REFERENCES ............................................................................ 291

BIBLE VERSIONS ..................................................................................... 291
BOOKS ..................................................................................................... 291
ADDITIONAL RESOURCES ....................................................................... 292

# ENDORSEMENT

El-Elyon is a faithful God and He loves us very dearly and it is through our obedience to His word He can entrust us with His blessings. Obedience is submission to another's authority, in this case God's authority. Many people don't realise that God's blessings are based on obedience! To be able to fulfil what we need to do in these last days we need to be in sync with God and to know and obey His will for our lives.

The same way every child would love and respect their earthly parents, we should all respect and honour our Heavenly Father so that it would be well with us. This book is going to be a big blessing to everyone who reads it.

**Dr Mojisola Adeyoyin**
*Dental Specialist*

# DEDICATION

I want to thank and appreciate God Almighty Elohiym who trusted me and granted me the grace to write this book for Him. He made it possible from the start to the end of this book. He is forever faithful, so I dedicate this book to the Almighty God our Father and our Lord and Saviour, Yahusha Ha-Mashiach.

# ACKNOWLEDGEMENTS

I cannot believe how God Almighty Elohiym can turn things around for His name to be glorified. When the Holy Spirit asked me to write this book, I was a bit sceptical because I haven't gotten any idea about writing a book and also based on the title. But I thank God for granting me the grace to write this book. It wasn't an easy project, but with the help of people, this project has now become a reality. So, I want to first of all thank God Almighty for trusting me to write this book.

I also want to thank my wonderful husband, Adam Mitchell, for being there for me, encouraging me till I finished this book. And my lovely children David Mitchell and Michael Mitchell for their support. I love you all and I pray that God Almighty continues to bless and prosper you all and uphold you with His mighty right hand. Amen.

I want to also thank my sister, Virginia Nzeribe, and my brothers Samuel, Emmanuel, and Mark for all their prayers. And I also want to thank my pastors, Paul Lloyd and His wife, Vicky Lloyd for your prayers and support. I love you both; May God Almighty continue to strengthen you and grant you grace to finish what He has commissioned you to do.

I want to also appreciate and thank Dr Mojisola Adeyoyin, seven-time bestselling Author Sister Adeyinka Adekunle-Kilani, Anatalie Duncan-John and

Sister Belinda Kanema from the bottom of my heart, I thank you all for all your effort, your love, your prayers, you all went the extra mile to ensure that this book is being published; May God Almighty continue to bless and prosper you all beyond your wildest dreams Amen.

I also want to thank and appreciate Dave Charles for the design of the book cover; I want to acknowledge and appreciate my publisher, Joy of many generations, for their hard work to make sure this book becomes a reality, may God Almighty continue to bless and increase you all in the Mighty name of LORD Jesus Christ Ha-Mashiach. Amen.

And finally, to everyone whom I have not mentioned, who were involved in one way or the other, I thank you all, may God bless you all in the mighty name of our LORD and Saviour Yahusha Elohiym Amen.

# FOREWORD

I met Sophia in an unconventional way at a time when I was seeking answers from heaven. The relationship grew quickly in a prayer-filled and professional manner. I quickly saw that her desire to care for and help others was at the forefront of her service to me and my daughter.

Fast forward to 17 months later, and Sophia was by my side during a crisis again, albeit virtually, in a prayer-filled, caring, authentic, and Holy Spirit-driven capacity. Furthermore, her commitment to surrender and faithfulness was evident in every aspect of her ministry.

This woman loves the LORD Jesus Christ, and it shows in her devotion to living according to Scripture. Consequently, when I learned of her being called to write this book, even though it was over the phone, the smile that emanated from her words motivated me and encouraged me to be willingly obedient amidst my own trials.

Moreover, this book, "Total Obedience" is an expression of Sophia's calling by the LORD God Elohiym. To say she was faithful in writing this is an understatement, as it was not just her faithfulness to content but to the utterances of the Holy Spirit, who I believe used Sophia to document direction and information directly from the open heaven to equip all who walk in the Christian faith and want to please Elohiym.

As Sophia so eloquently shares in this book, surrendering to God's will is the key to unlocking a life of true freedom, purpose, and fulfilment. Additionally, through her teachings, Sophia guides readers on a journey of obedience and, ultimately, liberation from the bondage of sin and self into a life of victory and intimacy with God Elohiym.

I'm certain this book will be translated into many foreign languages to meet the needs it was birthed and intended to. That is, for the world to know what being obedient is, why it is important, and how to demonstrate total obedience in their daily walk with God Adonai.

Once read, it can be used to continue to develop the believer's skills and spiritual muscle by revisiting it again to top up. Similarly, like the Bible, reading it during one season in your life will show one aspect, then re-reading it, you will learn something that was previously overlooked. It speaks specifically to your needs.

Whether you are agnostic, atheist, curious about God Elohiym, new following God's ways, the purpose of this book will be that which meets the needs of the reader, transforming lives as only something inspired by the Creator can do.

Sophia's ministry is a testament to her love for God and His people. Meanwhile, her experiences have given her the competencies to know what it is to seek God with her whole heart and sojourn until she meets Him.

I'm genuinely excited at the impact this manuscript will have on mankind. I am humbled and honoured to be able to write my thoughts on the book.

To my sister Sophia, may God bless you, and cause His face to shine on you. Be gracious to you and keep you in perfect peace. It's a blessing to call you sister and friend.

**Anatalie Duncan-John**

# PREFACE

I love the LORD Jesus Christ and truly want my life to reflect His glory. How do I fully walk in obedience to His word? What happens when I follow Him halfway? Sophia takes on this amazing journey of Total Obedience to our Heavenly Father, she explores hindrances to completely obeying Him.

Her wealth of experience from years of counselling and her passion for intercession birthed this book. She aims to ignite our passion to fulfil purpose on this side of eternity! This book is a powerful tool in the hands of a believer. You will read it and be filled with the love to obey and be fully transformed into the image of God.

It will equip you for the race and energise you for the prize ahead!

1 Corinthians 9:24 says: "Do you not know that in a race all the runners run, but only one gets the prize? Run in such a way as to get the prize." (NIV)

Get ready for an exciting journey of spiritual growth with this amazing book.

**Adeyinka Adekunle-Kilani**
*Seven-time Bestselling Author*

# INTRODUCTION

The fundamental laws of God El-Elyon are to structure us, make us conform to His perfect will and purpose for our lives. His commandments are not to punish us but a blessing to us if we as His children abide by them. The word of God is the only truth we can rely on! There are so many words spoken by different religious leaders in the world that are contrary to God's word which have kept millions of their followers in bondage. But the true word of Yahuah Elohiym is a lamp that will guide you to live a life of total obedience to God and live a life of fulfilment.

Proverbs 3:1-8 says: "My son, do not forget my law, but let your heart keep my commands; for length of days and long life and peace they will add to you. Let not mercy and truth forsake you; Bind them around your neck, write them on the tablet of your heart, and so find favour and high esteem in the sight of God and man. Trust in the LORD God Almighty with all your heart and lean not on your own understanding; in all your ways acknowledge Him, and He shall direct your paths. Do not be wise in your own eyes; Fear God Almighty and depart from evil. It will be health to your flesh and strength to your bones.

Total obedience is what God Almighty Elohiym wants from all His children! It is through our obedience to His commandments that we can be shaped to become His sons and daughters and live a life of fulfilment. We have to strive continuously to conform to the things of God; that means we have to constantly study His word and apply it in our daily walk with Him. Today many believers are still living in bondage even though Jesus Christ Yahusha Ha-Mashiach has set them free! Because they have neglected to study the word of God in order to acquire knowledge and build a relationship with Him. What we are seeing today in the world is because people have neglected the truth; Most people prefer to live in darkness than to live in the light! Christ is our light and until we dwell in Him, we cannot obey His commandments which He has set before us, and we won't be able to live a life of total victory that will bring constant glory to His name.

Our complete obedience to His word is what empowers us to operate here on earth as His sons and daughters and live a life of fulfilment!

# CHAPTER ONE

# KNOWING THE TRUE GOD

Adonai, the Almighty God is love, and He is forever eternal! Before God created the universe, He existed before time! Elohiym has no beginning, and He has no end. There's only one God, the Creator of the whole world which we serve. From the beginning of creation in Genesis to Revelation, God refers to Himself as "us" which describes the doctrine of the Trinity. The word Trinity comes from "tri" three and "unity" meaning one. He is one and only true God! He is omniscient (all-knowing God), He is omnipotent (all powerful God), and He is Omnipresent (He is everywhere at the same time). He is forever Holy and merciful! He is a covenant keeping God, and He is faithful in all His ways. He is the unchangeable God! He is the same yesterday, today and forever. He is the judge of the whole earth. Whatever God has said in His word, He is faithful to bring it to pass.

It is impossible for us to obey God's commandments if we do not have full knowledge of who He is! When you know someone and have trust in that person, that is when the relationship with that person will become perfect, that means the law of honour and respect has to be in place. Likewise, our relationship with Elohiym can only be perfect when we have a full knowledge of who He is, trust Him and walk in complete obedience to His will for our lives. Living a life of total obedience to the only true God, who gave Himself as a ransom for our sins, shows that we love and honour Him; His commandments are the pathway that would guide us to walk faithfully in becoming who He has made us to be. When we have grasped the word of God, that is when we can clearly hear His voice and follow His instructions.

Ephesians 4:13-14 says: "Until we all attain to the unity of the faith and of the knowledge of the Son of God, to mature manhood, to the measure of the stature of the fullness of Christ, so that we may no longer be children, tossed to and fro by the waves and carried about by every wind of doctrine, by human cunning, by craftiness in deceitful schemes." (ESV)

We have to go deeper to know Him objectively, and it is through the knowledge that we have acquired that will make us experience Him subjectively. It is the Holy Spirit that would help us to understand the objective word of God and bring it to a believer's subjective experience: The logos and the rhema of God are both crucial in our Christian life. The more we understand the logos, the more God can speak instant words to us which is the rhema. His instant words in any circumstances lead us and turn us to Him when we pay attention to them, so as we navigate through the Scriptures, it is very crucial we yield to the Holy Spirit our Leader for Him to teach us and give us the revelation of the Scripture and the finished works of our LORD Jesus Christ.

Apostle Paul prayed for the saints in Ephesus in Ephesians 1:17-19: That the God of our LORD Jesus Christ, the Father of glory, may give to you the spirit of wisdom and revelation in the knowledge of Him, that the eyes of your understanding being enlightened; that you may know what is the hope of His calling, what are the riches of the glory of His inheritance in the saints, and what is the exceeding greatness of His power toward us who believe, according to the working of His mighty power.

Before we can dive into knowing what God's word is saying to us and how we can be faithful to them and apply them in our daily walk with Him, we need to know some of His attributes.

## The attributes of God

### His Faithfulness

The Almighty God Elohiym, the Creator of the universe, is a faithful God. Whatever He has written in His word, He is faithful to bring them to pass. It is through His faithfulness that He sent His only begotten Son Jesus Christ to die for us.

1 Corinthians 1:9 says, God is faithful, (He is reliable, trustworthy and ever true to His Promise-He can be depended on), and through Him you were called into fellowship with His Son, Jesus Christ our LORD. (AMP)

This is one of the stories in the Bible that really touches my heart and makes me understand that God can do anything for His children who are faithful to His word.

When the people of Moab saw the multitudes of the Israelites that came to camp in the plains of Moab, they were deeply afraid because they thought the Israelites came to take possession of their land, they have also heard how Elohiym fought their battles for them and how they have defeated all their enemies and have taken possession of their land. So, Moab met with their king, Balak, and told him about the children of God and planned on how to defeat them. He knew how much God loves them, and how He has fought all their battles for them; and it will not be possible for anyone to defeat them except they sin against Elohiym; and for them to sin against God, they have to be cursed, in order for them to sin against Elohiym.

So Balak invited Balaam to curse the people of God for them to sin and for God to turn His face against them so that the Moabites can defeat them in battle. So, Balaam prayed, and Elohiym the Almighty God asked him not to go because they are blessed. But even after God had spoken to Balaam not to go to Balak, he still went; Elohiym was angry at Balaam for not obeying His word; so as Balaam was going to meet with Balak, on his way the angel of the LORD God Elohiym came and stopped the donkey he was riding on and the donkey refused to move since the LORD God Almighty had stopped Him from moving forward; Balaam became so angry at the donkey because the donkey refused to move. Not realizing why the donkey stopped moving, Balaam struck the donkey thrice and the LORD God Almighty opened the mouth of the donkey, and the donkey replied back to Balaam.

As the donkey was angry, telling his master the reason why he cannot move; God opened the eyes of Balaam, and he saw the angel of the LORD God Elohiym and he was afraid, and he pleaded for mercy. Then Elohiym permitted him to go but only to do what He would ask him to do. So, Balaam went to meet with Balak the next day and Balak took him to the high places of Baal; and Balaam asked Balak to build seven altars and offer seven ram and bull! Balaam then went to seek the face of the LORD God, and God put His words in his mouth, to bless the people of Elohiym instead of cursing them. Each time Balak would ask Balaam to curse the children of Israel; the Scripture says, Elohiym would minister to Balaam and Balaam would end up blessing them instead of pronouncing a curse on them (Numbers 22:1-41), (Numbers 23:1-20), ( cf. Numbers 24:1-25).

Numbers 23:8-11: "How shall I curse whom God has not cursed? And how shall I denounce whom the LORD God has not denounced? For from the top of the rocks I see him, and from the hills I behold him; there!

A people dwelling alone, not reckoning itself among the nations. "Who can count the dust of Jacob, or number one-fourth of Israel? Let me die the death of the righteous, and let my end be like his!" Then Balak said to Balaam, "What have you done to me? I took you to curse my enemies, and look, you have blessed them bountifully!"

So, Balaam took up this oracle and said: "The utterance of Balaam the son of Beor, and the utterance of the man whose eyes are opened; The utterance of him who hears the words of God and has the knowledge of the Most High! Who sees the vision of the Almighty, who falls down with eyes wide open; "I see Him, but not now; I behold Him, but not near; A star shall come out of Jacob; A sceptre shall rise out of Israel, And batter the brow of Moab, And destroy all the sons of tumult. "And Edom shall be a possession; Seir also, his enemies, shall be a possession, While Israel does valiantly. Out of Jacob one shall have dominion and destroy the remains of the city." (Numbers 24:15-19).

Balaam still continued pronouncing curses on the enemies of God's children. After Balaam had cursed Balak and his people, he departed and went back to his place and Balak left with great disappointment. Why did Elohiym intervene for the children of Israel? Why didn't He allow Balaam to curse them? Despite their lack of faithfulness towards Him, God still remained faithful to His word. He had blessed them because of His covenant with Abraham (cf. Genesis 13:14-18).

This divine intervention showcases God's unwavering faithfulness to His promises. The protection and blessings they received were not due to their own actions but were rooted in God's covenant with Abraham. Abraham's faithfulness and obedience to God set the foundation for this divine favour. When God commanded Abraham to leave his father's house and journey to a land He would show him; Abraham obeyed without hesitation. He left his homeland with his wife and Lot, his nephew, and traveled to the land of Canaan (cf. Genesis 12:1-5). This act of obedience not only brought blessings to Abraham but also extended those blessings to his descendants. Through His faithfulness, God honoured His promise to Abraham, demonstrating that His word stands firm regardless of human shortcomings.

## Abraham faithfulness to God

When Abram was ninety-nine years old, the LORD God Elohiym appeared to Abram again and made an everlasting covenant with him and his descendants and changed his name from Abram to Abraham and also changed the name of his wife Sarai to Sarah (Genesis 17:1-27). God's promise to Abraham finally came to pass and here comes the final test for Abraham (cf. Genesis 21:1-4).

Abraham now had the promised son, Isaac, and God asked Abraham to sacrifice his long-awaited son, the son that he had in his old age whom he loved dearly and offer him as a burnt offering. Abraham never questioned God on His commandment; but rather He obeyed immediately! Why? Because Abraham had come to know who God is and he had trusted Him that he is a faithful God, and that God can never go against His words. He knew that this was a test, and he also knew that Elohiym is more than able to raise Isaac, his son, from the dead! He knew how God works because he has spent so many years in a relationship with God; and he had seen God faithfulness in his life on several occasions, so he knows God cannot fail him, because God had told him that through his seed, Isaac, his descendants would be blessed (Genesis 15:5), (cf. Genesis 17:19), (Genesis 21:12), (Genesis 22:1-14).

Genesis 22:7-8: And Isaac spoke unto Abraham, his father, and said, "My father: And he said, "Here I am, my son." And he said, "Behold the fire and the wood, but where is the lamb for an ascending smoke offering?" Abraham said, "My son, Elohiym will provide Himself a lamb for an ascending smoke offering." So they went, both of them together (CEPHER).

Abraham had so much faith in the Almighty Elohiym that immediately God asked him to offer Isaac his son as a burnt offering; he didn't refuse! He took his son and headed to the place God Almighty Elohiym asked him to go and sacrifice his son Isaac. Abraham was ready to do exactly what God had already done even before the foundation of the world. Jesus, the Lamb of God, had already been sacrificed for the sins of the people of the world (Revelation 13:8).

Abraham, because of his love and faithfulness to God's word, was ready to sacrifice his son Isaac to God. If Abraham wasn't faithful to God and kept His commandments, do you think Elohiym would have blessed him and his descendants with these kinds of blessings? Not at all! Because if He does, then He is no longer faithful to His word. Abraham was the only person in the Bible mentioned that was ready to offer his only promised son to God! And the Almighty God Elohim in response blessed him and not only him but all his descendants.

When you continually put your faith and trust in our LORD and Saviour Yahusha Ha-Mashiach, He will not only bless you, but He will have full confidence in you. You will become His friend, just like Abraham was his friend (John 15:14-15), (cf. James 2:23), (Isaiah 41:8), (2 Chronicles 20:7). And you know what it means to become God's friend: whatever thing He wants to do that concerns you, or in your family, or on this earth, He will first of all reveal it to you and ask your opinion before He can take any action. Just like when He wanted to destroy Sodom and Gomorrah in Genesis 18:17-19; He told Abraham, His friend, and Abraham went into dialogue with Him till God came to a conclusion on what to do.

Psalms 119:90 says: "Your faithfulness continues through all generations; you established the earth, and it endures."

The only way you can please God and live a life of fulfilment is when you know that Elohiym is a faithful God and walk with Him faithfully. This is when God will start revealing Himself to you step by step! And when God starts revealing Himself to you, that is when you become His friend and live a life of fulfilment.

Deuteronomy 7:9 says: Therefore, know that the LORD your God, He is God, the faithful God who keeps covenant and mercy for a thousand generations with those who love Him and keep His commandments. (NKJV)

Adonai is the same yesterday, today and forever, His faithfulness reaches out for all those who walk with Him faithfully. Abraham walked faithfully with God, and God showed His faithfulness to him and his descendants. Enoch walked faithfully with God and God honoured him, he was God's friend. Moses walked faithfully with Him, and he was God's friend and God honoured him; the Apostles walked faithfully with Elohiym, and they all became God's friends and lived a fulfilled life.

Everyone in the Bible that walked faithfully with God, Adonai turned their story around for good. I encourage you today as a believer to walk with God faithfully in all your conducts, that's the only way you can carry His presence and live a life of total victory. Whatever God has said in His word, that is what He will do; He cannot lie because He's not a man that He should lie! He is forever faithful to His word. As a believer, if you refuse to walk with God faithfully, you are depriving yourself of His presence and from living a life of fulfilment.

Numbers 23:19 says: "God is not a man, that He should lie, nor a son of man, that He should repent. Has He said, and will He not do? Or has He spoken, and will He not make it good?

It is His faithfulness and mercies that have brought us from darkness into His kingdom and have kept us still standing regardless of all our disobedience to His word, God does not change; He still remains faithful!

## His Holiness

Elohiym is a Holy God, and we are all created to imitate Him. The moment we give our lives to God; our body becomes His tabernacle! So, He expects us to walk in holiness. Living a holy life is what qualifies us to operate on this earth as kings and priests unto Him (cf. Revelation 12:5-6). Without us living a holy lifestyle, we cannot carry His presence and manifest His glory, which is what differentiates us from the world. If we are not carrying His presence, how can we live a life of fulfilment? The only way our prayers can be answered without any hindrances is when we honour and obey Yahusha Ha-Mashiach by living holy.

Satan can only obey and fear those who are living holy, because he is aware of God's law.

This was why he tempted Adam and Eve and tried to do the same thing to Jesus Christ. This is the reason God commanded us to live a life of holiness because He knows if we don't, we will not only be disobeying His laws, but also, we would be giving the devil full permission to enslave us. It is for our own good that we live holy as children of Elohyim, so that we can have and enjoy the fullness of His presence and manifest His glory.

1 Corinthians 3:16-17, Paul speaks: "Know ye not that ye are the Temple of Elohiym, and that the Spirit Elohiym dwells in you?" (CEPHER)

1 Peter 1:15-16 also says: "But as He which hath called you is Holy, so be ye holy in all manner of conversation; because it is written, be ye holy; for I Am Holy."

As followers of Yahusha Ha-Mashiach, it is very fundamental that we consciously live a life of holiness. God has called us out of darkness to represent Him on earth as His children! To renounce every work of darkness and accept to walk in the path of holiness that would bring honour and adoration to His Holy name. There is no way a believer can walk with God without keeping the law of holiness. Why did Elohiym Almighty destroy Sodom and Gomorrah? It was due to their immoral ways of living (Genesis 19:1-29).

Romans 12:1, Apostle Paul wrote: I appeal to you therefore, brethren, by the mercies of Elohiym, that ye present your bodies a living sacrifice, holy, acceptable unto Elohiym, which is your reasonable service. (CEPHER)

Many believers don't actually understand what it means to be holy! For them they believe as long as someone has accepted Christ as their Saviour and they are going to church, it's fine - even though they are still living a life of immorality. So, they continue to live in sin without repentance. This is the biggest lie of the devil, making people believe that as long as they are going to church, and they have accepted Jesus Christ as their Saviour they are saved. Let me tell you the truth; a believer that is not living a holy life is not saved! It is only when you obey His commandment by living holy that you are saved.

If someone that was a murderer or an idolater, or an homosexual, or adulterer before, now believes in Christ, and that person refuses to repent and continues living that kind of lifestyle, even though that person believes in Christ, if that person dies without repentance; that person cannot make it to heaven! And not only will such a person not make it to heaven, but also that person can never carry God's presence.

Each time in the Scripture Jesus healed someone; He would tell the person to go and sin no more, because sin is what opens the door for the enemies to come in and afflict us and separate us from God's presence. In John 8:1-11; we read how the Scribes and the Pharisees brought in a woman that was caught in adultery to Jesus and wanted to stone her, but Jesus showed compassion on her and intervened; He said if any among them that has not sinned should throw the first stone. The scribes and Pharisees, knowing that they were all guilty couldn't throw a stone at her and one by one they left the woman, and in verse 11, Jesus looked at the woman and told her to go and sin no more.

1 Corinthians 6:9-11 says: Do you not know that the unrighteous will not inherit the kingdom of God? Do not be deceived. Neither fornicators, nor adulterers, nor homosexuals, nor thieves, nor covetous, nor drunkards, nor revilers, nor extortioners will inherit the kingdom of God.

Hebrews 6:4-6 states: For concerning those who were once enlightened and tasted of the heavenly gift, and were made partakers of the Holy Spirit, and tasted the good word of God and the powers of the age to come, and then fell away, it is impossible to renew them again to repentance; seeing they crucify the Son of God for themselves again, and put Him to open shame. (MWB)

So don't be deceived! No one living to please the flesh can please Elohiym! God cannot go back on His word! Stop living a life of immorality that would only bring eternal death to your soul in hell. When someone is living a life of immorality, that person is still a slave to the devil and a slave cannot dwell in the presence of God and enjoy the fullness of His blessings. Only sons and daughters of Elohiym dwell in His presence! So be wise and walk in holiness before Yahuah Adonai because He loves and cares for you so dearly.

1 John 2:6 says: "Those who say they live in God should live their lives as Jesus did." (NLT)

# Job's confidence in God

Job was a man after Elohiym's heart! He was a righteous man! A man that feared God, to the extent that Elohiym boasted about him to Satan. Then the LORD God Almighty Adonai said to Satan, "Have you considered My servant Job, that there is none like him on the earth, a blameless and upright man, one who fears God and shuns evil?" (Job 1:7-8). According to Scriptures, God allowed Satan to try Job; but why would Elohiym do that? Because His sovereignty makes us understand that He knows everything about us, both past, present and future; therefore, when He tests us, it is not to see whether we will pass the test or not; rather His testing us is to take us to a higher level of His glory in order for us to manifest His kingdom on earth. Even though Job went through the fire, lost everything, his children and all his wealth initially, God restored double of everything he had lost; his latter end became very glorious!

Job 42:12-13: Now the LORD God Almighty blessed the latter days of Job more than his beginning; For he had fourteen thousand sheep, six thousand camels, one thousand yoke of oxen, and one thousand female donkeys. He also had seven sons and three daughters. (NKJV)

"Our holiness creates a gateway for God's presence being manifest in every area of our lives."

Revelation 4:8 says: And the four living creatures, each of them with six wings, are full of eyes all around and within, and day and night they never cease to say,

"Holy, holy, holy, is the LORD God Almighty, who was and is and is to come!"

    God's grace is available, so everyone who is struggling to live a life of holiness should ask Him for His grace. Make up your mind and be willing to make a change in your way of living, because it is only when you are willing to repent and turn away from your sin by renewing your mind and accepting the truth that He has set you free from sin and death, and that you are no longer a slave to sin but a child of the Most High God, you will start to live a life of holiness. Knowing the truth of who He is and who you are in Him, will set you free from being a slave to sin! He has set you apart! You cannot live and act the way people in the world are acting. So, cleanse yourself from all filthiness of the flesh and walk in holiness, because that is the only way your life would bring glory and honour to Him.

Matthew 5:48 says: Be ye therefore perfect, even as your Father which is in heaven is perfect.

John 17:16: Jesus when praying to the Father, said, "They are not of the world, just as I am not of the world."

The only way people of the world will come to know Jesus Christ Elohiym and accept Him as their LORD and Saviour is by the way we live because we are His representatives here on earth. We serve a Holy God, so we must consciously live a life that is holy, bringing glory and honour to His Holy name. Matthew 5:13-16 reminds us of who we are in Christ to this world. We are the salt of the earth, if we lose our saltiness, how can it be made salty again, it will be of no value again. We are the light of the world, to bring light to this dark world we are living in; if we belong to Him and we truly love Him, then we must strive to live to His standard of holiness, that is the only way our light can shine and for us to demonstrate His power.

1 Peter 2:9 says: "But you are a chosen generation, a royal priesthood, a holy nation, His own special people, that you may proclaim the praises of Him who called you out of darkness into His marvellous light.

Any minister that is preaching the gospel but is living an ungodly lifestyle can never be used and empowered by God. Elohiym can only empower those who are honouring Him with their way of living; because our holiness is a worship to God, so if we are not living holy, we cannot worship Him in spirit and in truth! That is why it is hard for ministers who are not living holy to bear good fruit. Every fruit will produce its kind! A good fruit will always produce its kind, and a bad fruit will always produce its kind. The only way we can produce good fruit for the kingdom of God and for us to live a life of fulfilment, is when we follow God's way, by living holy (John 15:1- 8).

You can never take authority over the devil, until you're living holy! And that's why most ministers of the gospel have sold their souls to the devil! They are going to the devil to bargain with him for power, because they are unable to keep to God's commandments and manifest His power and do what God initially called them to do. Elohiym has a standard! He will not reduce His standard of Holiness, because some people can't keep to His standard. We have to strive to live to God's standard of holiness because His grace is available to help us overcome sin. The word of Elohiym is more than able to change us and transform us to become whom He has called us to become. The more time we spend in His word, and in prayers, seeking Him, the more grace we will receive to live a life of holiness as He is Holy.

1 Thessalonians 5:22 says: "Abstain from all forms of evil (withdraw and keep away from it)" AMP.

## His Power

Throughout the Scriptures we have read how the Almighty God Elohim demonstrated His power, and even now we see God's power being manifest everywhere, even in our own lives. He made the heavens and the earth by His great power! His understanding is infinite! By His power, He knows the number of the stars and calls them all by their names. It takes power to create the world, and most importantly, humans. In Genesis 1:1-31, God demonstrated His divine power when He created the whole world; He rules by His power forever, there is none like our God Elohiym throughout the whole universe!

Isaiah 52:10 says: "The LORD has demonstrated His holy power before the eyes of all the nations. All the ends of the earth will see the victory of our God."

Revelation 4:11 says: Thou art worthy, O LORD God Almighty, to receive glory and honour and power, for thou hast created all things, and for Thy pleasure they are and were created. (KJV)

Psalms 62:11 says: God hath spoken once; twice have I heard this, that power belongeth unto God. (KJV)

The God of Abraham, Isaac, and Jacob that we serve and worship is a great God! His greatness is unsearchable. The greatness of God speaks of His absolute rule over all things. His endless resources, His incredible power to do as He pleases and for whomever He pleases.

In Isaiah 40:25-26, God asks: "To whom then will you liken Me, or to whom shall I be equal?" says the Holy One. Lift up your eyes on high, and see who has created these things, who brings out their host by number; He calls them all by name, by the greatness of His might and the strength of His power; not one is missing.

2 Peter 1:3 states: Seeing that His divine power has granted to us everything pertaining to life and godliness, through the true knowledge of Him who called us by His own glory and excellence.

God's greatness is immeasurable! "I am" is His name; He is Omnipresent, Omniscient, Omnipotent. Yahuah Elohiym- the Most High God. He is Sovereign, there is nothing hard for Him to do. The reason why most believers don't take God seriously is because they haven't experienced His divine power in their life. So, they find it very difficult to trust Him completely and even to share the gospel of Jesus Christ with others because they have not encountered His power. For you to preach the gospel, you yourself must have experienced His power in your life, and so you're very convinced that Jesus Christ is who He said He is and the only way to salvation.

Your personal encounter with God is very important, because without your personal encounter with Him, you cannot be firm in your faith and tell others who He is, because you haven't had any experience with His divine power in your life; and that is why most believers are confused! They're lukewarm (Revelation 3:15-16). If the body of Christ cannot demonstrate God's power, how would there be a revival? How can we change the ungodly system of this world? To change the systems of the nations of this world, we need to demonstrate the power of Elohiym. That is the reason we were called to be His ambassadors. We were not called to bear titles but to represent Him by demonstrating His kingdom on this earth.

1 Corinthians 2:4-5, Paul says: "And my speech and my preaching were not with persuasive words of human wisdom, but in demonstration of the Spirit and of power, that your faith should not be in the wisdom of men but in the power of God."

Apostle Paul, laboured day and night for the gospel, to experience the power of Jesus Christ and His resurrection and to demonstrate it! Until you take God and the gospel of our LORD God and Saviour Yahusha seriously, you will not experience the divine power of Elohiym in your life and to express it to others.

1 Thessalonians 2:9, Apostle Paul wrote: For you remember, brethren, our labour and toil; for labouring night and day, that we might not be a

burden to any of you, we preached to you the gospel of God.

Believers all over the world are preaching the letters of Apostle Paul, because he paid the price of knowing the true God Elohiym and to demonstrate His divine power. A man that was persecuting believers before, got arrested by Ha-Mashiach on His way to persecute the followers of Jesus, and Paul became a new man. He did not just repent and give his life to the Messiah Yahusha, but he was completely sold out to the gospel and God demonstrated His power in his life and through him. It is only when we are dead to the things of this world and faithfully carry our cross daily to follow Him that He can empower us to rule as kings and priests on this earth. Yes, we will make heaven as long as we have accepted Him as our LORD and Saviour and are living for Him; but to rule as kings and priests, we have to carry our cross daily and follow Him faithfully!

Philippians 3:10, Apostle Paul wrote: "That I may know Him and the power of His resurrection, and the fellowship of His sufferings, being conformed to His death."

We have read throughout the Scriptures how Elohiym demonstrated His power. How He brought plagues to the land of Egypt and destroyed Pharaoh and his men in the red sea (Exodus chapters 7 to 14).

Romans 1:20, Paul wrote: For since the creation of the world, His invisible attributes, His eternal power and divine nature, have been clearly seen, being understood through what has been made, so that they are without excuse.

So, as children of the Most High God, we have no excuse not to live a life of constant victory, walk in and demonstrate His divine power, because the world is waiting to see the manifestation of the power and glory of God Elohiym on this earth.

## His Words

God's word is eternal! They stand firm in the heavens and on this earth. He spoke His word and the whole world was created. His words concerning us can never be changed; they are powerful and sharper than any double-edged sword. The word of Elohiym is our foundation on which we stand on; our spiritual growth depends on the knowledge we have of His word. The only thing that would make His word not to be fulfilled in our life is when we disobey His laws.

Matthew 24:35, Jesus speaks: Heaven and earth will pass away, but My words will by no means pass away.

Until God's word dwells in your spirit and becomes part of you, you will be tossed to and fro being deceived by the evil ones! Whenever you are praying, it is through His word you can be able to pray effectively! Because whenever you are praying, it is the word of

God in you that the Holy Spirit would bring to your remembrance; without the Scriptures in you, the Holy Spirit cannot speak the rhema to you because you don't have the logos in you. The rhema word can also be received while studying the Bible! For instance, you are studying the word of Elohiym and you come across a Scripture, the Holy Spirit will instantly minister to you with that Scripture, and you will know at that instant that that word is for you.

So, studying the word of God is very vital for our spiritual growth and for our everyday life on earth. In Matthew 4:1-11, when Satan came to tempt Jesus at three different times, the Bible said Jesus responded by telling the devil, "It is written" at each time! And the devil left Him alone. Jesus could have just ignored the devil and walked away, and nothing would've happened, because He is God Elohiym, but Jesus replied to the devil with His word. Why? So that we would do the same, living by the living word of God.

Romans 15:4 says: For whatever things were written before were written for our learning, that through perseverance and through encouragement of the Scriptures we might have hope.

The reason why most believers are victims of the devil, is because they lack the revelation of God's word! They read the Bible with no understanding, because they are just reading it without inviting the Holy Spirit to teach them. That is why they function like everyone else in the world! The only way you can understand the Scriptures is when the Holy Spirit is the one teaching you. Most believers think the devil is their problem; they don't know that the devil was defeated long ago when Christ came, died, resurrected and made a public show of him and all his cohorts. Elohiym has given every believer power over all principalities and powers! The devil knows this truth except some believers that are too lazy to study the word of God in order to know the truth of the finished works of Yahusha Ha-Mashiach on the cross, so that they can operate in the fullness of the power of the Holy Spirit.

When you see believers that have been born again for many years and are still going from one pastor to another, from one social media platform to another, seeking for prayers, looking for deliverance, know that such people are still far from knowing the truth. As a child of the Most High God, you don't need to be delivered anymore, because you are already delivered. All you need is to acquire knowledge of His word. He is already in you, whatever things in your life that you want to change, you can change it through the word of Elohiym.

Make out time to know God through His word and build a relationship with Him. Any situation that you might be facing, you will come out of it eventually if you abide in His word and have faith in Him. Remember, without faith, no one can please Him and receive anything from Him. Faith is what empowers the word of God in your mouth that you have declared. Allow the Holy Spirit to guide you into all truth, learn how to pray and sometimes fast! Let the word of Adonai be part of you, this is how to grow spiritually and operate in the power of Elohiym and have a good relationship with Him.

If you only rely on a pastor to hear what Elohiym is saying, then you have a serious problem! Because you don't know if what your pastor is telling you is the truth or not. So, as a believer you should learn how to hear your heavenly Father's voice. Jesus said in John 10:27: "My sheep hear My voice, and I know them, and they follow Me." You can only follow Him if you can hear His voice, if you cannot hear His voice, how can you follow Him in the direction He is leading you to and keep His commandments? So, this is why you need to know God's word for yourself so that you can be able to hear His voice; without His word in you, you cannot keep His laws and live a constant life of victory! It is the level of your understanding of His word that would help you to stand firm in faith in case you face any trials or temptations.

Matthew 7:14, Jesus speaks: "Therefore everyone who hears these words of mine and puts them into practice is like a wise man who built his house on a rock."

The only way God's word can be effective in your life is when you constantly study them, abide by them and put them into practice; this is how to live a life of fulfilment. Going from one social media platform to another seeking help is not the best thing to do. If you don't know the word of Elohiym and build your relationship with Him, you will fall into the wrong hands; because there are so many false ministers that have camouflage themselves as angels of light misleading people to the devil. You need discernment to be able to discern which spirit they are operating from! So, sit down, study God's word and understand it, build your relationship with the Holy Spirit, so that you can walk in the truth and live a life of fulfilment. The pastor you are depending on is also depending on Elohiym, so study the Scriptures to be approved by God.

Proverbs 4:20-22, God speaks: My son, give attention to my words; Incline your ear to My sayings. Do not let them depart from your eyes; Keep them in the midst of your heart; For they are life to those who find them, and health to all their flesh.

"There are four principles we need to maintain: First, read the word of Elohiym! Second, consume the word of God until it consumes you. Third, believe the word of God! Fourth, act on the word." (Smith Wigglesworth)

## His Glory

Our LORD and Saviour Yahusha is the king of glory! His glory cannot be compared to anything in the entire world! His glory is far beyond any human's description; God's glory is above all the heavens and the earth. The glory of Elohiym is the magnificence, worth and splendour of God's character and attributes. His glory is the manifestation of His greatness, beauty, and perfection, which is greater than our imagination. It is His glory in our lives that would set us apart and make the world know that we are His children. Without His glory in our lives, we are like everyone else in the world, being oppressed by the enemies, not able to enjoy the glorious life that Yahusha Ha-Mashiach died for us to live! We were created to show forth His glory and that is the way He is glorified —When we are living a life full of His glory.

Isaiah 49:3 says: And He said to me, "You are My servant, O Israel, in whom I will be glorified."

Psalms 8:1 says: O Yahuah Adonai, how excellent is your name in all the earth, who has set Your glory above the heavens. (CEPHER)

Psalms 19:1 says: The heavens declare the glory of God, and the firmament shows His handiwork.

In Exodus 34:28-35: We read how Moses spent forty days and forty nights on Mount Sinai, being in the presence of the LORD God Almighty Adonai! And Moses' face became so shining, covered with the glory of Elohiym; Moses had to cover his face with a veil each time he wanted to talk to the children of Israel, and whenever he wanted to talk to God, he would then remove the veil from his face. God's presence is so powerful that when you constantly spend time in His presence, His glory will begin to manifest in your life.

The reason there's no revival in all the cities and nations of the world is because the magnificence and glory of God is missing in the body of Christ because of disobedience! The Bible says anywhere Ha-Mashiach went, multitude followed Him! In Acts 2:1-41: The Bible says, on the day of Pentecost, when the Apostles received the Holy Spirit, they started speaking in tongues, in different languages and that day more than three thousand people gave their lives to Yahusha! There was a great revival that day. Why? Because they followed Yahusha instructions, they were obedient to His word. So, for us to see revival in our nations, in our cities, we need to abide by His laws to manifest His glory. Until believers repent and follow the ways of Elohiym and seek His face continually, we will still not operate in the power of God the way the Apostles in the Bible operated. There are believers everywhere, but it's as if there are no believers at all, because there are just few good shepherds in the world to guide God's people to the truth, for them to become sons and daughters of the Most High God Elohiym.

Matthew 9:37, Jesus said to His disciples, "The harvest is abundant, but the workers are few." (CSB)

No matter how good a preacher or anyone can preach, if that preacher does not carry the glory of Elohiym, that person is preaching in vain. People's hearts will still be hardened, and there will be no repentance. And this is why our cities, and the nations of the world are filled up with drug addicts, witchcraft, occults, and all kinds of immoralities, because the body of Jesus Christ has refused to totally surrender to God's commandments. Compare the early believers in the book of Acts with those of today, can you see the difference? My fellow brothers and sisters in Christ, we have to keep to God's commandments if we want to see the move of Elohiym in this generation.

If believers cannot live by the word of God; How do we think God's glory will manifest? He is a Holy God! He told us to be holy if we want to carry His presence and manifest His glory. He alone is our LORD and God; we need His glory to change the situations of things that are surrounding us! We need His glory to be poured out on this earth, for wickedness to cease and lives to be transformed from darkness to light. So, believers all over the world have a great responsibility to do what the Apostles of Jesus Christ and the Prophets did that changed history!

Habakkuk 2:14 says: For the earth will be filled with the knowledge of the glory of the LORD God Almighty, as waters cover the sea!

This should be our assignment, till we all see the glory of our LORD God and Saviour cover the whole earth! We should keep on striving in the spirit.

## His Presence

Elohiym's presence is not limited by time or space! He is Omnipresent, He is present everywhere at all times. Whenever we find ourselves in any situation, God's presence is always with us, guiding and protecting us, whether we feel Him or we don't feel Him at all. As long as we are His children, we should be rest assured that He will always be with us. It is His presence that would make a difference in our life! Without His divine presence, it will be impossible for anyone to do what God has called him or her to do. Experiencing the presence of Elohiym is very vital for our wellbeing, spirit, soul and body! It is only in His presence we can find true peace, love, joy and strength to live in this evil and wicked world. When we abide in His presence, that is when we would be transformed, from glory to glory!

Matthew 28:20b says: "I am with you always, even to the end of the age."

God's presence is always there! But we need to walk in accordance with His will for us to dwell and remain in His presence and live a life of fulfilment. The reason why most children of Elohiym are not operating in His power, even after Jesus Christ has said in His word that He has given us power to tread upon serpents and scorpions and over all the powers of the enemies and nothing shall by any means harm us (Luke 10:19), and they are still living in fear, is because they don't have a relationship with the Holy Spirit. They don't carry His divine presence! Believers all over the world are over 2.5 billion, and it's as if we are just few; darkness is taking over the earth!

The Apostles were just twelve, but look at all the great signs and wonders they did in their time? Because they carried the presence of the living God Elohiym! They had a relationship with the Holy Spirit! Everyone in the Bible that manifested the power of Elohiym, carried His divine presence. It is God's presence that you carry that would put your enemies to silence; whatever thing you are looking for, it is in His presence that you can receive it. It's God's presence that you carry that would bring total protection to your life and that of your loved ones. You will always triumph over your enemies when you carry God's presence.

Psalm 16:11 says: You will show me the path of life; in Your presence is fullness of joy; At Your right hand are pleasures forever.

Psalm 97:7 says: "The mountains melt like wax at the presence of the Lord God Almighty; at the presence of the Almighty God of the whole earth."

Psalm 27:4 says: "One thing I have desired of the LORD God Almighty, that will I seek; that I may dwell in the house of the LORD all the days of my life; to behold the beauty of the LORD God, and to inquire in His temple."

It is in the presence of Elohiym, you will experience His mighty power and manifest His glory. Stop spending time binding the devil all morning and all night without the presence of God. If you are not living a holy life and keeping His commandments, it will be hard for you to live a life of victory. Those that are living holy are the ones that are carrying the divine presence of Elohiym. Today there are all sorts of deliverance ministries all over the world, binding and casting out devils, and the more they are binding and casting demons, the more the powers of darkness are invading the earth! Why? Because you can only bind and cast out devils when you are in a relationship with Elohiym; when you are living holy! That is when God will honour His words in your mouth.

Mark 16:17-18, Jesus speaks: And these signs will follow those who believe: In My name they will cast out demons; they will speak with new tongues; they will take up serpents; and if they drink anything deadly, it will by no means hurt them; they will lay hands on the sick, and they will recover."

Matthew 6:33 says: Seek ye first the kingdom of Elohiym, and His righteousness, and all these things shall be added unto you (CEPHER). Seek His presence, which is the secret key for manifesting His glory and power in your life.

Moses said to Elohiym, if your presence will not go with us, do not bring us up from here. Because he knew how important God's presence is! He knows without God's presence; they cannot survive and make it to the promised land (cf. Exodus 33:14-15). Likewise, without God's presence in your life, you cannot make it to the promised land.

# God's love for us

In John 10:11-18, Jesus speaks: "I am the good shepherd. The good shepherd gives His life for the sheep. But a hireling, he who is not the shepherd, one who does not own the sheep, sees the wolf coming and leaves the sheep and flees; and the wolf catches the sheep and scatters them. The hireling flees because he is a hireling and does not care about the sheep. I am the good shepherd; and I know My sheep and I am known by My own. As the Father knows Me, even so I know the Father; and I Lay down My life for the sheep. And other sheep I have which are not of this fold; them also I must bring, and they will hear My voice; and there will be one flock and one shepherd. Therefore, My Father loves Me, because I lay down My life that I may take it again. No one takes it from Me, but I lay it down of Myself. I have power to lay it down, and I have power to take it again. This command I have received from My Father."

No matter how much you have messed up in life, Yahusha Ha-Mashiach still loves you with unconditional love! And He wants to have a relationship with you! Every parent loves their children, irrespective of what they've done. No matter how badly a child behaves, the parent will never turn their back on that child, rather they would do everything for that child to become a better person. If humans that are wicked know how to show love, how much more Elohiym Yahusha whose nature is love! It is because of His love for us that compelled Him to come and die for our sins. This is the greatest and the highest love anyone can give, to lay down his or her life for someone; but Yahusha Ha-Mashiach did it for the whole world, so it is left for you to believe in Him and accept this great love and live for Him.

Romans 5:8 says: But Elohiym commends His love towards us, in that, while we were yet sinners, Mashiach died for us (CEPHER).

"There is no greater love than this love, that God will send His only Son Ha-Mashiach to come and die for the sins of the world so that we would not perish but be in His presence forever even when we leave this world, for eternity." (John 3:16)

## The Prodigal son

The story of the prodigal son is a story that demonstrates God's unconditional love towards us. The son asks his father for his inheritance, then travels to a distant country and squanders it in wild living. After he had spent all his money, there was a severe famine in that country, and he was looking for means to survive, he came to a point where he wanted to feed on pigs' food. The Bible says, one day he came to his senses that he could not continue to live in such an unclean and unholy lifestyle, that he would rather return to his father and be one of his father's servants! So, he returned, and from a far distance when the father saw him, he was filled with compassion and ran to him, embraced him and brought him home. "The son said to his father, 'I have sinned against heaven and against you. I am no longer worthy to be called your son.' But the father, filled with joy, said to his servants, 'Quick! Go bring the best robe and put it on him!' He then put his ring on his finger and sandals on his feet. He asked them to bring the fattened calf and kill it! 'Let's have a feast and celebrate. For this son of mine was dead and is alive again; he was lost and now he is found' (Luke 15:11-30).

This story tells us how deeply Yahuah Elohiym loves us! You do not need to be ashamed of your past sins or mistakes, or try to become a better person first before you come to Him, because on your own, you can never become a better person; the only way you will become a better person is through Jesus Christ our Messiah. God wants you to know that He did not come for the man that claims to be righteous but for sinners. Once you realise that God's love is a precious gift to be treasured, you will run to Him and cling to His love.

## God's amazing grace

The Apostle Paul's story is another story in the Bible that demonstrates God's amazing grace. Apostle Paul, a murderer, going about persecuting the Christians found God's mercy on his way to persecute the Christians, the Messiah Jesus Christ appeared to him and that was how Apostle Paul was transformed and became one of the great men that God used in the Bible (Acts 8:3), (cf. Acts 9:1-20).

1 Corinthians 15:9-10, Paul speaks: For I am the least of the Apostles, who am not worthy to be called an Apostle, because I persecuted the church of God. But by the grace of God, I am what I am, and His grace toward me was not in vain; but I laboured more abundantly than they all, yet not I, but the grace of God which was with me.

When Apostle Paul came to realise the abundance of God's grace and love, he diligently sought for it until he found it. He never compromised his faith; he was diligently seeking to know Yahusha Ha- Mashiach who had called him out of darkness so as to serve Him faithfully. So, as a believer seek Him diligently till you see His glory in your life and in this generation.

Ephesians 3:8-9, Paul wrote: "To me, I am less than the least of all the saints, this grace was given, that I should preach among the Gentiles the unsearchable riches of Christ, and to make all see what is the fellowship of the mystery, which from the beginning of the ages has been hidden in God who created all things through Jesus Christ.

## God's love on the criminal on the cross

The criminal on the cross beside Jesus Christ that was about to make hell his everlasting home, met God's abundance of love and grace. All his criminal records were deleted within a second and he went to heaven where all the saints are, who have laboured so hard to get there, he just got there by God's abundance of love and mercy (Luke 23:39-43)

One of the criminals who was hanged insulted Him, saying, "If You are the Messiah, save Yourself and us." But the other, answered, and rebuked him and said, "Don't you even fear God, seeing you are under the same condemnation? And we indeed justly, for we receive the due reward of our deeds; but this Man has done nothing wrong." Then he said to Jesus, "LORD, remember me when You come into Your Kingdom." And Jesus said to him, "Assuredly, I say to you, today you will be with Me in Paradise" (Luke 23:39-43).

The reason one of the criminals was saved instantly and went to heaven was because he discerned that the man among them was an innocent man that didn't deserve to die. He believed that this was the Messiah! Even when people were making mockery of Him, he believed that Jesus Christ is the Messiah. And the saddest thing is that most of the people that were in the crowd that were shouting, "crucify Him!" have seen all the great miracles that Jesus Christ did; some of them had received their healing, still they rejected and abandoned Him with no gratitude; wicked hearts! But this criminal that just met Him, never knew anything about Jesus, never saw any of the miracles that He did, yet believed in Him that He is the Messiah and asked Him to have mercy on him and remember him when He goes to heaven.

And this was how his faith took him to heaven while the other criminal went to hell because he refused to believe the truth and repent. The reason the Apostles could do great and mighty miracles was because they understood the greatness of God's abundance of love and grace and they were completely obedient to Him. They sought Elohiym the Most High God with all their heart, in good times and in bad times. Abraham understood God's love and that was why he could trust Him totally and Elohiym blessed him beyond his wildest dream.

For any believer to operate in the supernatural realm and do great things on this earth for the kingdom of God, that person has to understand the abundance of God's love and surrender completely to His commandments. And until we understand God's love for us, we cannot love Him and love others and keep His laws; we can only demonstrate our love for Him by obeying His commandments.

1 John 4:16 says: And we have known and believed the love that God has for us. God is love, and he who abides in love abides in God, and God in him.

All the other commandments of God are fulfilled on this commandment written in Matthew 22:37-40: Jesus said to him, "'You shall love the LORD your God with all your heart, with all your soul, and with all your mind.' This is the first and greatest commandment. And the second is like it: 'You shall love your neighbour as yourself.' On these two commandments hang all the laws and the Prophets."

So, we should all continue to strive to abide in His love and demonstrate the love of Christ to unbelievers, this is the only way the body of Jesus Christ will manifest His glory and power and win souls for Him.

# CHAPTER TWO

# TOTAL OBEDIENCE TO GOD

Jesus Christ Himself when He was on this earth, demonstrated His obedience to the Father! He who had always been God by nature, did not cling to His prerogatives as God's equal, but stripped Himself of all privileges by consenting to be a slave by nature and being born as mortal Man. And having become Man; He humbled Himself by living a life of total obedience, even to the extent of dying, and the death He died was the death of a common criminal. And He urges us to do the same by keeping His commandments.

That is why the Bible says, God has highly lifted Him, and has given Him the name beyond all names, so that at the name of Jesus Christ "every knee shall bow," whether in Heaven or earth or under the earth. And that is why, in the end, "every tongue shall confess that Jesus Christ is the LORD" to the glory of God the Father. (Philippians 2:5-11), (cf. Isaiah 53:3-11)

Do you know what it means for Elohiym the Most High God to bring Himself to this earth in the form of a human, just to pay the price for our sins? He went through all the insults, mockery, all the humiliation, the rejection from His own people. The Father led Him to be tempted by the devil that He Himself created. The people that He created spat on Him, flogged Him, they blasphemed Him, and persecuted Him on the cross for doing no wrong; the only wrong He did was to come and bear the sins of the whole world, the sin that Adam and Eve committed (cf. Genesis 3:1-7). He totally surrendered to the Father's will!

John 8:28-29: Then Jesus therefore said to them, "When you lift up the Son of man, then you will know that I am He, and that I do nothing of Myself; but as My Father taught Me, I say these things. He who sent Me is with Me. The Father hasn't left Me alone, for I always do those things that are pleasing to Him."

1 John 2:3-4 says: "And we can be sure that we know Him if we obey His commandments. If someone claims, "I know God," but doesn't obey God's commandments, that person is a liar and is not living in the truth." (NLT)

    The reason God the Father Yahuah was completely pleased with Jesus the Messiah is His total obedience! Yahusha Ha-Mashiach was totally obedient to the will of the Father God Elohiym Yahuah for His life. When Jesus was about to finish His ministry; He was in the garden of Gethsemane praying and He said to the Father the same prayers three times. "O Father, if it is possible, let this cup pass from Me, nevertheless, yet not as I will, but as you will." (cf. Matthew 26:39-44).

Since you have received Jesus Christ as your Lord and Saviour; walk in total obedience, have faith in His word so that you can be able to live a life full of His glory.

## Our obedience is what honours God

Our obedience to God shows that we love and honour Him. It is our obedience to His commandments that enable us to dwell in His presence, manifest His glory and live a life of fulfilment. If Jesus Christ being God Elohiym had to submit Himself to the Father's will in order to reconcile us back to the Father Yahuah and fulfil His own purpose here on earth, then we have no excuse not to submit our lives totally to God's will, for us to be in a perfect relationship with Him and bring glory and honour to His Holy name. Remember a servant is not greater than His master! Without God's commandments we will be lost, we will be confused, and we will live a lawless life and be separated from His presence forever!

The most important commandment that Jesus Christ laid down for us to keep is the commandment written in Matthew 22:37-40: "You shall love the LORD your God with all your heart, with all soul, and with all your mind. This is the first and greatest commandment. And the second is like it: 'You shall love your neighbour as yourself.' On these two commandments hang all the law and the Prophets."

As believers, if we say we love Yahusha Ha-Mashiach, and we are not living a life of obedience to his word then we are liars. 1 Corinthians 6:20 says: "For you were bought at a price; therefore, glorify God in your body and in your spirit, which are God's." Living a consecrated life and a sacrificial life unto God is what opens the doors of our inheritance in Christ; if you're ignorant of God's word, you will be ignorant of His will for your life. When we keep His commandments, that is when our lives can make a meaning on this earth! Keeping His commandments is having faith in Him! Allowing the Holy Spirit to be our teacher to guide us through His word.

One of the ways to show that we love and honour God is by loving others. And this is where many believers are lacking! Even in the house of God, you will see competitions, envy, strife, gossip, hatred! Now can God be honoured by someone who is operating in the flesh? Not at all! God can only be honoured by someone who is operating in the fruit of the spirit, which is love, joy, peace, patience, kindness, goodness, faithfulness, gentleness, and self-control (Galatians 5:22-23). So, before we can say we love and honour God, let's show love to people we can see physically, not to talk down on people! By doing this, we can then be assured that we are obeying God's word.

1 John 4:20-21 says: If someone says, "I love God," and hates his brother, he is a liar; for he who does not love his brother whom he has seen, how can he love God

whom he has not seen? And this commandment we have from Him: That he who loves God must love his brother also.

His commandments are easy to follow if we yield to His word! We are created in His image to do great things in this earth for His glory; so if we have to do the things He has called us to do, then we have to be totally obedient to His laws, be imitators of Jesus Christ our Saviour who did not come to this earth to please Himself but the Father Yahuah; likewise, we are here in this earth to please our Heavenly Father and His purpose for our lives.

James 1:22-25, Apostle James speaks: But be doers of the word, and not hearers only, deluding your own selves. For if anyone is a hearer of the word and not a doer, he is like a man looking at his natural face in a mirror; for he sees himself, and goes away, and immediately forgets what kind of man he was. But he who looks into the perfect Torah (law) of freedom and continues, not being a hearer who forgets but a doer of the work, this man will be blessed in what he does.

"God is awesome; He doesn't need you to be awesome; He needs you to be obedient." (Matt Chandler).

# The light shines even in the darkest moments

Joseph was another great man that feared the Almighty God Elohim and honoured Him! He was a man of integrity! A righteous man that loved God. Genesis chapters 37 to 48 tell us what Joseph went through to get to where God Elohiym has destined him to be. Even though Joseph knew that he had a great destiny based on his dreams, he never knew the processes! Most Christians today would not want to go through the process that Joseph had to go through to pass the test of obedience and become what God has created them to be. The Bible says, his brothers were jealous of him, because of his dream, so they conspired against him to kill him! Later they changed their mind and threw him into a pit! Afterwards, they sold him to the Ishmaelites for twenty shekels of silver.

The brothers then went home, told their father Jacob that Joseph was killed by a wild animal. Then the Midianites sold him to Potiphar, an Egyptian, an officer of Pharaoh and captain of the guard. All this while God Almighty Elohiym was with Joseph and God blessed all that Joseph did, and Potiphar seeing that God was with Joseph, promoted him as he saw the hand of God upon Joseph's life. And Potiphar made him overseer of his house and all that he had, and God blessed Potiphar's house for the sake of Joseph.

Then in chapter 39:1-20, we read how Potiphar's wife tried to have sex with Joseph on several occasions, but Joseph refused because he feared and honoured

God and because of that she lied against him and Potiphar sent him to prison. Joseph in all these trials, never sinned against God; he was faithful to God, trusting Him, keeping His commandments, knowing that one day Elohiym will vindicate him! And even in the prison God's presence was with him, and Joseph found favour in the eyes of the prison guard, and the prison guard made Joseph the head over all the other prisoners because of the way Joseph presented himself in the prison. And it came to pass that the butler and the baker of the king of Egypt offended the king, so they were sent to the same prison where Joseph was (Genesis:40:1-3).

And it came to pass that both of the king's men had a dream and Joseph happened to interpret the dreams for them! Later, what Joseph told them concerning their dreams came to pass. The butler returned back to his office while the baker's head was cut off by Pharaoh (Verse 8-22). Even when Joseph asked the butler to remember him when he was released, he forgot about Joseph; Joseph continued to remain faithful to God, trusting that one day, God Elohiym will vindicate him! Joseph spent more than two years in prison for a crime he never committed. Pharaoh later had a dream and needed someone to interpret the dream for him but found none.

It was at that moment the butler remembered Joseph, how he interpreted their dreams and it came to pass, he now told Pharaoh that he knew someone who could interpret his dream for him and that was how Pharaoh invited Joseph to his palace and Joseph interpreted Pharaoh's dream and advised Pharaoh on what to do concerning the dream. Pharaoh saw that God was with Joseph for him to interpret his dream that none of his oneirocritic could interpret, and was very pleased with Joseph and he made Joseph the prime minister of the land of Egypt. Joseph was in charge of the whole land of Egypt, that whatever he said was what the king did. And all of Joseph's family came to Egypt because of the famine in the land of Canaan. He became so wealthy and famous, but despite all these blessings and honour in his life, Joseph never allowed pride to take over him, he never stopped worshipping Elohiym; and he never got angry at his brothers, rather he showed them great love and he was completely faithful to God until he died (Genesis chapters 37-50).

Everything Joseph said to Pharaoh about his dream came to pass, the hand of the LORD God Almighty Elohiym was mightily on Joseph because of his obedience to Him. See how God allowed Joseph to walk through the trials, to test his obedience! But the more Joseph faced the trials and temptations, the more his faith in God increased. Joseph's dream of his brother's sheaves bowing down to his sheaves all came to pass and all his family came to Egypt due to the famine in the land and he became their ruler.

This is what obedience to Elohiym's commandments does! Joseph wouldn't have fulfilled his purpose if he had disobeyed God's commandments and had refused the pruning; he rejected sin and stayed focused on God alone! Man looks at the outward appearance, but God looks at the heart of a man. How many people would behave like Joseph, trusting God in the midst of trials? How many people will still love their brothers or sisters after they have done terrible things to them? All these stories written in the Bible are not just fiction, they are events that actually happened so that we can all learn from them.

"Great faith is the product of great fights! Great testimonies are the outcome of great tests. Great triumphs can only come out of great trials." (Smith Wigglesworth)

1 Samuel 2:30b says: "But now the LORD says: 'Far be it from Me; for those who honour Me I will honour, and those who despise Me shall be lightly esteemed."

The whole earth is waiting for the manifestations of the sons of the Most High God Elohiym. How can we manifest the glory of Yahusha Ha-Mashiach in our life when we cannot keep His commandments? The whole creation is crying for the manifestations of God's glory! Heaven and earth are waiting; who will manifest the glory of God in this generation? Because this generation is the last generation before the Messiah returns, and we know through Scriptures that the coming back of our LORD Yahusha Ha-Mashiach is at hand.

1 Peter 4:7-11 wrote: The end of all things is at hand; therefore, be serious and watchful in your prayers.

And above all things, have fervent love for one another, for "love will cover a multitude of sins." Be hospitable to one another without grumbling. As each one has received a gift, minister it to one another, as good stewards of the manifold grace of God. If anyone speaks, let him speak as the oracles of God. If anyone ministers, let him do it as with the ability which God supplies, that in all things God may be glorified through Yeshua (Jesus Christ) to whom belong the glory and the dominion forever, Amen (WMB).

## Obedience to surrender to His will

Are you willing to say, "Elohiym, let Your will be done in my life and not my will," even though His will is to take you out of your comfort zone? Are you ready to give up your dreams and follow God's dreams for your life? Are you ready to carry your cross and follow Him even unto death? Are you ready to pay the price for the sake of the gospel? Jesus Christ said to the young man in Matthew 19:21 to go sell all his possessions and give the money to the poor, the young man was disappointed and walked away because he had great possessions. For any believer to be a friend of God Elohiym, that person has to die to the flesh daily and carry his cross.

John 15:14-17, Jesus speaks: You are My friends if you do whatever I command you. No longer do I call you servants, for a servant does not know what his master is doing; but I have called you friends, for all things that I heard from My Father I have made known to you. You did not choose Me, but I chose you and appointed you that you should go and bear fruit, and that your fruit should remain, that whatever you ask the Father in My name He may give you. These things I command you, that you love one another.

We can only bear fruit for the kingdom of God when we walk in total obedience to His commandments; living a holy life and seeking Him continually! This is the only way our light will shine, going from glory to glory and winning souls for His kingdom. In the tapestry of life, the word of God is the bridge that would guide and help you to cross the tempestuous storm that is fierce against you, leading to arrive at your destiny. If you do not abide by His word and follow His will for your life, how will you live a life of fulfilment? He said in His word in Jeremiah 29:11, "For I know the plans I have for you, declares the LORD, plans to prosper you and not to harm you, plans to give you hope and a future.

Deuteronomy 28:1-2 says: "Now it shall come to pass, if you diligently obey the voice of the LORD your God, to observe carefully all His commandments which I command you today, that the LORD your God will set you high above all nations of the earth. And all these blessings shall come upon you and overtake you, because you obey the voice of the LORD your God.

The reason this earth remains the way it is, is because most believers have refused to be the light of the world. No matter how dark a house is, when you switch on the light, instantly the whole house will be luminated with light. Likewise, if we are carrying the presence of the Most High God, no darkness can be able to stand against us. When the light shines, darkness has to flee! But darkness can only flee when we are carrying His light by obeying His commandments.

Most preachers are preaching how to make wealth but refusing to preach how to study the word of Elohiym and be obedient to God's commandments; no child of God can be blessed without total obedience to His word! That is why when I see ministers of the gospel preaching about prosperity, without preaching how to totally surrender to the ways of the Holy Spirit, it makes me feel really sad; if you are still living in the flesh, it will be hard for you to carry God's presence and operate in the supernatural. Elohiym is a Spirit and everyone who worships Him has to connect with Him in the Spirit! Obeying His commandments is the only way we can carry His presence and operate as kings and priests and live a life of fulfilment! You cannot bribe God with your money, the only way to carry His presence is total obedience to His words.

## Beyond words

Another significant person I want to talk about is Mary the mother of Yahusha Ha-Mashiach when He was on this earth as human. As believers we know that God Elohiym is a Spirit, and a Spirit cannot die for our sins. So, for God to carry out His plan to pay the price for our sins and reconcile us back to Himself; He had to take the form of a human to die for our sins. So, for Him to accomplish that, He has to come through the womb of a virgin and be born as a child; because He is a Holy God, and it is only a holy person that can pay the price, He came through Mary because she was God fearing and a devoted virgin; if He came through the same ways humans are being born into this world, then He will be like every other person born into this earth, as a sinner! That means, He can no longer be a Holy God to save humans. Because it is only a holy person that is qualified to save humans from the penalty of sin which is death.

Romans 5:18 says: Therefore, as through one man's offence judgement came to all men, resulting in condemnation, even so through one Man's righteous act the free gift came to all men, resulting in justification of life.

Mary was a virgin at the time angel Gabriel appeared to her and told her the good news that she will conceive and give birth to the Messiah.

Luke 1:30-33 wrote: And the angel said unto her, Fear not, Miryam (Mary): for you have found favor with Elohiym. And, behold, you shall conceive in your womb, and bring forth a Son, and shall call His name Yahusha. He shall be great, and shall be called the Son of El Elyon: and Yahuah Elohiym shall give unto Him the throne of His father David. And He shall reign over the house of Jacob forever; and of His kingdom there shall be no end (CEPHER).

Mary knew fully well that no one would believe her story that she conceived by the power of the Holy Spirit; she knew the stigma that would be on her, she knew the rejection and abandonment that would follow by her family members, friends and neighbours; she knew she won't be allowed into the temple of the Most High God anymore! And that Joseph, her fiancé would end up not marrying her and probably she might be stoned to death!

All these were in her mind; she already knew how the situation would change her life, in the sense that she was a virgin not married yet and would be pregnant with a child. Mary instead of not having faith in God and focusing on the difficult situations that looked so impossible that she would be facing responded to the angel; "Behold the maidservant of the LORD! Let it be to me according to your word." And the angel departed from her (Luke 1:26-38).

Mary was completely obedient to the will of God Adonai for her life even though it wasn't her will. She was ready to face whatever situation that would arise even unto death. That is the kind of obedience and faith God is looking for; someone that would surrender to

His will completely, trusting Him completely beyond all odds. There were many virgins at that time in the city of Galilee that Elohiym would have visited, but God Adonai decided to choose Mary to use her womb to come to this earth to die for all humans in order to reconcile us back to Himself.

So why would God choose Mary among all the other virgins to be the woman that would give birth to Him? Because Mary was a very devoted God-fearing woman! She had great faith, and she had a pure heart. Matthew 5:8 says: "Blessed are the pure in heart, for they shall see God." Mary was highly favoured by God because of the pureness of her heart and total obedience to His word! She was living a consecrated life.

Luke 1:28: "Rejoice, highly favoured one, the Lord God is with you; blessed are you among women!"

Today, believers all over the world honour and celebrate her because of how God honoured her. Today if only you will harken to the voice of the LORD Your God, you will be the next person God will favour and honour in this generation.

The same way God searched in Israel and found Mary; Yahusha Ha-Mashiach is earnestly looking for people He will empower to do His work here on earth. Those that would totally surrender to His will and say here I am My LORD and Saviour, send me. And as you completely surrender to His will for your life, He will honour you and make the world to celebrate you.

Matthew 19:29 Jesus speaks: "And everyone who has left houses or brothers or sisters or father or mother or wife or children or lands, for My name's sake, shall receive a hundredfold, and inherit eternal life."

When God Almighty Elohiym said I will bless you for obeying Me, He meant it! God never made a promise and failed! All through the Scriptures, we have read the faithfulness of Elohiym to those who obeyed His commandments and accepted His will for their lives. So, as you walk with Him and keep His commandments, He will show His faithfulness in your life, because He is forever faithful.

Proverbs 16:20 says: He who pays attention to the word (of God) will find good, and blessed (happy, prosperous, to be admired) is he who trusts (confidently) in the Lord. (AMP)

Romans 8:19 says: "For the earnest expectation of the creature waiteth for the manifestation of the sons of God."

The world is waiting for who will be the next Moses, who refused to be called the son of Pharaoh's daughter; choosing rather to suffer affliction with the people of God, than to enjoy the pleasures of sin for a season; esteeming the reproach of Christ greater than the treasures in Egypt! Who will be the next Daniel, who refused to listen to the king's commandments but continued praying to God knowing fully well that the punishment is death! Who will be the next great Prophets in the Old Testament, that God used mightily!

Who will be the next Abraham that was ready to sacrifice his beloved son Isaac to God Yahuah Elohiym! Who became God's best friend! Who will be the next Mary Magdalene who was faithful to Jesus Christ, and she was the first woman Jesus Christ appeared to when He resurrected from death! Who will be the next three Hebrew men that were ready to die than to bow to king Nebuchadnezzar's image and were thrown into the fiery fire and Yahusha Elohiym was with them in the fire, and He preserved them! Who will be the next Apostles of Jesus the Messiah, who brought the kingdom of God down to earth, the watchmen of those days.

All these are faithful people who lived a life of total obedience to God's will (cf. Hebrews 11:4-12); and they demonstrated the power of God in their time, and until now the whole world is still talking about the mighty things that God Elohiym did through these great men and women of God in the Scriptures.

John 14:12-14, Jesus speaks: "Most assuredly, I say to you, whoever believes in Me, the works that I do he will do also; and greater works than these he will do, because I go to My Father. And whatever you ask in My name, that I will do, that the Father may be glorified in the Son. If you ask anything in My name, I will do.

Jesus Christ assured us that when we keep His commandments, He will do whatever thing we ask the Father in His name according to His will for our lives. So, are we asking Him? No! We are not asking Him in faith and in total obedience. Believe me, the reason most believers are not able to operate in the gifts of the Holy Spirit and be filled with the fruit of the Spirit is because they refuse to obey Elohiym's commandments. Any child that doesn't love their parents will never obey their parents. Likewise, you can only keep God's laws when you love Him (John 14:21).

"If you love me, keep My commandments. And I will pray to the Father, and He will give you another Helper, that He may abide with you forever, the Spirit of truth, whom the world cannot receive, because it neither sees Him nor knows Him; but you know Him, for He dwells with you and will be in you. I will not leave you orphans; I will come to you. John 14:15-18 (NKJV)

## Our obedience compels Him to be faithful towards us

It's our complete obedience to His word that will compel Him to do extraordinary things in our lives. If we are not doing our part in honouring His word in our lives, how do we expect Him to honour His word in our lives? Two can only walk together when they agree; the Scriptures that we quote can only bear fruit in our lives and to others when we humble ourselves and walk in the fear of the LORD God Almighty Elohiym. Someone that fears the Almighty God Yahuah will not live a life of immorality, the person will be very conscious of the presence of the Holy Spirit, not to grieve Him, and even when mistakenly the person falls into sin, the person will humble himself and repent immediately.

We are all human, the only perfect Person is Elohiym, but we have to constantly examine ourselves so that we would always be in sync with His word in order to fulfil His plans and purpose for our lives. Many people go to church because of His blessings, not because they love Him and want to have a relationship with Him. That is why they're always looking for prosperity preachers! Many ministers opened churches not because they love to work in His vineyard but because of what they will gain from it.

Abraham's faithfulness compelled Elohiym to bless him and his entire generations! God Elohiym is a faithful God! He will never fail you nor forsake you, when you keep His commandments. He will bless you and extend His blessings to your generations if you obey His word and surrender completely to Him. When I say blessings, I am not talking about financial blessings; I am talking about His divine presence that brings His supernatural peace, and supernatural supply: You become His friend! So many believers are enjoying the blessings of God Yahusha Ha-Mashiach in their lives because of the faithfulness of their parents towards Elohiym Yahuah and His commandments.

Deuteronomy 30:19-20: I call the heavens and earth to record this day against you, that I have set before you life and death, blessing and cursing; therefore choose life, that both you and your seed may live; that you may love Yahuah Elohiym and that you may obey His voice, and that you may cling unto Him for He is your life, and the length of your days; that you may dwell in the land which Yahuah swore unto your fathers, to Abraham, Isaac, and Jacob, to give them. (CEPHER)

Luke 11:28: Jesus speaks: "More than that, blessed are those who hear the word of God and keep it!"

Proverbs 3:1-2 wrote: "My son, do not forget My teaching, but let your heart keep My commandments; for length of days and years of life (worth living) and tranquillity and prosperity (the wholeness of life's blessings) they will add to you". (AMP)

## Disobedience to God's commandments is dangerous

Disobedience to God's commandments is a sin before God Elohiym. When the Almighty God Adonai created man, He said "Let Us" make man in Our image, according to Our likeness (Genesis 1:26); since God is holy and faithful, He never breaks any of His commandments, likewise He expects us to do the same in order to be in a perfect relationship with Him. As soon as God created Adam and Eve and put them in the garden, He instructed them not to eat of the tree of knowledge of good and evil (Genesis 2:17).

Instead of them to obey Elohiym the Most High Sovereign God their maker and continue to enjoy His presence, they went against His instructions and did the unthinkable thing by willingly obeying the words of the devil which brought total separation and spiritual death to them and to the entire world. When God brought the children of Israel out from Egypt and made them pass through the wilderness in order to test their faith, they failed the test, and all of that generation died in the wilderness except their children who did not sin.

Joshua 5:6 says: For the children of Israel walked forty years in the wilderness, till all the people who were men of war, who came out of Egypt, were consumed, because they did not obey the voice of the LORD-to whom the LORD swore that He would not show them the land which the LORD had sworn to their fathers that He would give us, "a land flowing with milk and honey."

Isaiah 48:18 says: "Oh, that you had listened to my commands! Then you would have had peace flowing like a gentle river and righteousness rolling over you like waves in the sea," (NLT)

There are always consequences when we disobey Elohiym's commandments! When someone rebels against God's commandments; it brings a curse to that person, and sometimes to that person's generation if the generation does not repent and seek God. Many believers are suffering today because their parents rebelled against God and due to that, curse came into their life. And instead of them to diligently seek God, studying His word so that they will acquire knowledge and be in a perfect relationship with Elohiym and break free from the bondage; they are going from church to church looking for deliverance ministers that would deliver them; not wanting to know God Yahusha for themselves so that they can hear His voice and follow His instruction and come out from the oppression.

And most times they end up in the wrong hands that will put them into more spiritual bondage! Because we are in the end time and many people that claim to be ministers of God are actually working for the devil. So, you need great discernment to be able to discern these wolves that are pretending to be God's servants. I was once a victim to these false Satanic ministers! So, I am writing to you based on my personal experience. My grandmother from my father's side was an idol worshipper; and because I wasn't living a life of total obedience, those evil forces were having the upper hand over my life.

So that was how I started looking for a deliverance minister that would help me, instead of me to repent and seek Elohiym's face, and study His words and know Him personally so that I can walk in total victory; I was just going from one pastor to Prophets to Apostles, to bishops; But each one I met, as soon as the minister would lay his hands on my head and pray for me, things would become rather worse instead of me being delivered. It happened to me a few times with different prominent ministers, so one day I made up my mind and said enough is enough!

I want to know God for myself. So, I went on my knees, and I repented of my disobedience and started to seek Him, and that was how I started studying the Scriptures so that I will know Him and have a relationship with Him. And since I started following His instructions, His gifts in my life have manifested. I can hear His voice clearly and obey Him! I can now enjoy His presence in my life. Even though sometimes challenges will come, I am still at peace, knowing that the Almighty God Elohiym Yahuah is by my side always; nothing shakes me since I started walking with the Holy Spirit. Of course, the devil will always try to see if he will succeed but I never allow him to put any fear in me because that's his greatest weapon.

Every day of my life, I am enjoying the presence of the Holy Spirit, and I can never trade Him for any amount of wealth! His presence is what we all need to be able to live in perfect peace! I thank God Almighty Elohiym for everything because if not for my experience, I wouldn't have had the knowledge to write this book.

Therefore, not studying the word of Elohiym can make you not to live a life of obedience; because without His word, you cannot hear His voice clearly to follow His instructions. The reason many believers are living a life of immorality is because they are not acquainted with God's word; if you can have time to read all sorts of non- Christian books and watch all sorts of worldly Tv programmes and movies, and you don't have time for God's word, then you're not obeying His commandments. Anyone who disobeys God's commandments cannot live a life of fulfilment! The consequences of disobeying God's commandments can be very dreadful (cf. Deuteronomy 28:15-68).

Look at what happened to Adam and Eve, they lost the most precious thing in their life; they were once enjoying the presence of Elohiym and were in total control of everything God created and put in the garden, the next minute they were in extreme darkness (Eternal death) because of disobedience. The Bible says in Romans 6:23: the wages of sin is death. The reason why many people are perishing in the world and are going to hell is because they have decided to turn their back on God Yahusha Ha-Mashiach, the one who created all things!

"Our disobedience deprives us from God's presence, and eternal life with Him." There are always consequences for the bad choices we make. (cf. Deuteronomy 28:15-68).

The Bible says in Mark 8:36: What will it profit a man if he gains the whole world and loses his own soul; our soul is very important to God, therefore it should be very important to us as well. There are so many witchcraft practices in the body of Christ now! The spirit of Leviathan has taken over most churches in the world today! People are worshipping demons, and they pretend to be worshipping the Most High God, but they are in the church to destroy God's people. Elohiym has given us free will to choose which path to take, either the path that leads to death or the path that leads to eternal life.

Satan cannot give anything good to anyone but death, so repent now and surrender to Jesus Christ who has all the powers in Heaven and on the earth and beneath the earth. The whole world belongs to Him and Him alone! There is judgement after death and if you have not reconciled with Him by accepting Him as your LORD and Saviour, it will be really bad for you when you leave this earth because everyone will one day leave this earth and face the Creator of the universe whose name is Yahusha Ha-Mashiach.

Hebrews 9:27 says: And as it is appointed unto men once to die, but after this the judgement.

There are so many believers who still believe and follow the ways of the world even when they have read it in Scriptures not to be conformed to the things of this world but to renew their mind through the word of Elohiym and be approved by Him; they rather follow the ways of the people of the world and grieve the Holy Spirit. We are to separate ourselves from every paganism; A person that's disobedient to God's commandments cannot dwell in His presence. Each time we disobey God's commandments without repentance, it will be hard for us to operate as sons and daughters in our calling and make heaven.

I have come across believers, who still enjoy the pleasures of this world, doing things unbelievers are doing, going places unbelievers are going, talking the way unbelievers are talking, dressing the way unbelievers are dressing, lovers of self instead of lovers of Elohiym the Almighty God! Repent now and do what is pleasing to God so that you can carry His presence and manifest His glory.

Romans 12:2 says: And do not be conformed to this world ( any longer with its superficial values and customs ), but be transformed and progressively changed ( as you mature spiritually ) by the renewing of your mind ( focusing on godly values and ethical attitudes), so that you may prove ( for yourselves ) what the will of God is, that which is good and acceptable and perfect ( in His plan and purpose for you ).

Colossians 2 says: Beware lest any man spoil you through philosophy and vain deceit, after the tradition of men, after the rudiments of the world, and not after Christ.

2 Timothy 3:1-5 says: But know this, that in the last days perilous times will come: For men will be lovers of themselves, lovers of money, boasters, proud, blasphemers, disobedient to parents, unthankful, unholy, unloving, unforgiving, slanderers, without self-control, brutal, despisers of good, traitors, headstrong, haughty, lovers of pleasure rather than

lovers of God, having a form of godliness but denying its power. And from such people turn away!

Revelation 22:14-15 says: Blessed are those who do His commandments, that they may have the right to the tree of life and may enter through the gates into the city. But outside are dogs and sorcerers and sexually immoral and murderers, and whoever loves and practises a lie.

Revelation 22:12 says: "And behold, I am coming quickly, and My reward is with Me, to give to everyone according to his work."

"The heart that has really tasted the grace of Christ, will instinctively HATE sin." (J.C. Ryle).

## How to be obedient to God Elohiym

First thing you need to do is to believe in Yahusha Ha-Mashiach, that He came to this earth to die for the sins of the whole world, and then confess your sins to Him, after that, you invite Him into your life as your LORD and Savour. Romans 10:9 says: That if you confess with your mouth the LORD Yahusha Ha-Mashiach and believe in your heart that God has raised Him from the dead, you will be saved. "Whoever believes in Him will not be put to shame." And begin to spend quality time studying His word. Do not waiver! Make a decision; do it now before it is too late.

## Prayer of Confession

"Dear LORD Yahusha Ha-Mashiach, I believe that You are the Messiah, and that You came to this earth to die for my sins, I am sorry for all of my sins, I confess them to you, and I repent of them all. I confess You as My LORD and Saviour, may You cleanse me with Your precious blood and make me whole. My LORD and Saviour Yahusha, may You come into my heart and life and live in me, fill me with your Holy Spirit, from now onwards I will live for You and keep to Your commandments by the help of the Holy Spirit in me. Thank You My LORD and Saviour Yahusha for saving my life and soul from eternal death and giving me eternal life to be with You forever" Amen.

Now that you are born again, the second thing to do is to pray to God Elohiym to guide you to a true God-believing church that preaches the word of God and practises it. After that, attend Bible class or beginners' class and study the Bible. Begin to study the word of Elohiym, and put them into practice, make it a habit, meditate on the word of God, let it become part of you; begin to learn how to pray and fast. As you continue to obey the word of Elohiym, you will begin to grow in the spirit, and that is how you become filled with the Spirit of God and begin to do extraordinary things in God's kingdom. Your life will never remain the same again as you start to obey God's commandments, I see you manifesting His glory and power in the mighty name of our LORD and Saviour Yahusha. Amen.

# CHAPTER THREE

# UNDERSTANDING YOUR PRIESTHOOD

As believers we are all called by God Almighty Elohiym to be anointed and become His priests and kings that would stand in the gap for sinners. The reason for a priesthood is to change the ways things are on this earth to the ways of Elohiym. This office is very significant in God's kingdom on this earth; because everyone whom God has brought out from the kingdom of darkness is to operate in this office. People who have gained God's trust and Adonai have been empowered are the ones operating in this office, even though this priesthood office is meant for all God's children to operate.

In the Old Testament, the Bible mentioned Melchizedek as the first priest that was operating in the priesthood as Jesus Christ "For this Melchizedek, king of Salem, priest of the most High God, who met Abraham returning from the slaughter of the kings and blessed him, to whom also Abraham gave a tenth part of all, first being translated "King of righteousness," and then also King of Salem, meaning "King of peace," without father, without mother, without genealogy, having neither beginning of days nor end of life, but made like the Son of God, remains a priest continually Hebrews 7:1-3 (NKJV).

Revelation 12:6 says: "And has made us kings and priests to His God and Father, to Him be glory and dominion forever and ever Amen.

1 Peter 2:9 says: But you are a chosen generation, a royal priesthood, a holy nation, His own special people, that you may proclaim the praises of Him who called you out of darkness into His marvellous light.

Hebrews 2:17 says: Therefore, in all things He had to be made like His brethren, that He might be a merciful and faithful High Priest in the things pertaining to God, to make propitiation for the sins of the people.

Jesus Christ is our High Priest, so for us to fulfil our priesthood calling, we must look unto Him alone and walk worthy of Him who has called us into His kingdom and glory. We should heed to the priesthood office which we have received from our LORD Jesus Christ and walk faithfully to fulfil it. Elohiym has ordained us to be His workmanship, so that through us, the manifold wisdom of God might be made known to the world and bring glory and honour to His Holy name alone.

1 Peter 2:4-5 says: Coming to Him as to a living stone, rejected indeed by men, but chosen by God and precious, you also, as living stones, are being built up

a spiritual house, a holy priesthood, to offer up spiritual sacrifices acceptable to God through Jesus Christ the Messiah.

Today in Christianity, you can only find a few believers operating in different dimensions of the office of the priesthood. Most believers don't understand the reason why God brought them out of darkness to become His sons and daughters. Many ministers now are operating under the priesthood of Baal, instead of operating according to the order of Melchizedek, under the priesthood of Christ. They have left their purpose! They have become the priest of Satan, fulfilling his wicked plans on earth. The reason Yahusha came to this earth to die is to reconcile all humans back to the Father Yahuah and become His vessels and be light to this dying world.

## Our mission here on earth

Our mandate on this earth is soul winning, this is the only way God can empower us as His sons and daughters to operate in the office of the priesthood. For your light to shine and impart lives, you must be on fire for Elohiym, you must put God above everything else in your life. Look at John the Baptist, he was a burning and a shining light (John 5:35). John the Baptist was a true witness; he was operating in the supernatural power of God! Because of the authority and power he was operating at, the Jews had to send priests and Levites to ask him who he was. And he said to them "I am 'The voice of one crying in the wilderness: Make straight the way of the LORD." John 1:23.

Matthew 28:19-20, Jesus speaks: "Therefore go and make disciples of all nations, baptizing them in the name of the Father and of the Son and of the Holy Spirit, and teaching them to obey everything I have commanded you. And surely, I am with you always."

Do you think if John the Baptist was after his own gain, God Elohiym would've empowered him? Jesus Christ came to be baptised by John the Baptist; were there no other Prophets at that time? Of course, they were! But because of John's total obedience to God, Elohiym empowered Him to be His witness. He was so bold to the extent that he said to Herod about Herodias, his brother Philip's wife, that "It is not lawful for him to have her as a wife. Today how many ministers of the gospel will stand up and speak the truth. Look at immoralities everywhere in the church, the church that Jesus Christ bought with His precious blood: It is only those that are true sons of Elohiym that have the boldness to preach against immoralities! These are the true witnesses of Christ, and these are the believers God empowers to represent Him here on this earth.

Acts 1:8, Jesus says: "But you will receive power when the Holy Spirit has come upon you, and you will be My witness in Jerusalem and in all Judea and Samaria, and to the end of the earth."

Ephesians 6:19-20: Apostle Paul asks the believers in Ephesus to pray for him so that he will be bold to speak the truth always without compromising. "Pray for me, that utterance may be given to me in opening my mouth, to make known with boldness the mystery of the good news, for which I am an ambassador in chains; that in it I may speak boldly, as I ought to speak. (WMB)

Before any believer can speak boldly the true gospel of Jesus Christ, that person must totally surrender to the Holy Spirit! Spend quality time in His presence seeking His face in the place of prayer to be empowered by Him. This is why we need genuine intercessors in the church to stand in the gap for ministers of the gospel of Jesus Christ. Some ministers of the gospel and some members of the congregation are after what they will gain from God rather than what they'll do to honour and glorify His Holy name. For God Yahusha to come down to this earth to die for humanity, know that people are very precious to Him! The reason He created us, is for His glory.

Isaiah 43:7 says: "Everyone who is called by My name, Whom I have created for My glory; I have formed him, yes, I have made him." He created us to glorify Him, to show forth His glory.

## It's all about Elohiym

The gospel is not about prosperity! It's about Christ, His birth, death, and resurrection; the gospel is the good news that God has accomplished through Jesus Christ to bring about the salvation of all who repent and believe in Him. It is about doing and fulfilling what Christ came to die on this earth! The reason He brought us out of darkness is to represent Him on earth, and do His will; the same way Jesus Christ changed the identities of His disciples from being fishermen to become fishers of men; that's the same thing He wants to do with us, to be fishers of men for His kingdom. So, in everything we are doing, we should do it in order to bring glory to His name.

He didn't ask us to seek after the things of the world that unbelievers are seeking or doing; He asked us to seek His kingdom and by seeking His kingdom, He will then bless us with whatever we need. Today most believers are boasting about their wealth instead of making disciples for Christ. That's why in most churches today, you will see a lot of babies instead of sons and daughters that would operate under the priesthood of Christ; because there are only a few genuine shepherds that would teach and guide God's children in the truth of God's word.

Matthew 6:33 says: "But seek first the kingdom of God and His righteousness and all these things shall be added to you.

Galatians 6:14, Apostle Paul speaks: "But far be it from me to boast except in the cross of our Lord Jesus Christ, through which the world has been crucified to me, and I to the world.

Apostle Paul speaks in his letters in 2 Corinthians 11:22-30: Are they Hebrews? So am I. Are they Israelites? So am I. Are they ministers of Christ? -I speak as a fool-I am more: in labours more abundant, in stripes above measure, in prisons more frequently, in deaths often. From the Jews five times I received forty stripes minus one. Three times I was beaten with rods; once I was stoned; three times I was shipwrecked; a night and a day I have been in the deep; in journeys often, in perils of waters, in perils of my countrymen, in perils of the Gentiles, in perils in the city, in perils in the wilderness, in perils in the sea, in perils among false brethren; in weariness and toil. In sleeplessness often, in hunger and thirst, in fasting often, in cold and nakedness. Besides the other things, what comes upon me daily: my deep concern for all the churches. Who is weak, and I am not weak? Who is made to stumble, and I do not burn with indignation? If I must boast, I will boast in the things which concern my infirmity.

No wonder our LORD Yahusha Ha-Mashiach empowered Apostle Paul to do what he did in his time, and the whole world is reading his letters today, and preaching from them. The abominations of this generation are far worse than the days of Sodom and Gomorrah, because there are not enough believers that are willing to carry their cross. Most preachers didn't wait upon the LORD God Elohiym to be taught and be processed before they went and opened churches. That's why they fell into the hands of Satan! The youths are perishing, people are going to hell! Will you blame them? Or we the body of Christ should be blamed for not doing what we were called to do as disciples of Jesus Christ!

We are His witness; He has commissioned us to go and represent Him everywhere He has sent us, but most people have abandoned what they first believed and are now doing what they think is best for them. They find it difficult to speak the truth and stand by it; they are after the things of the world, instead of being the kings and priests God had called them to be!

Jesus said in Matthew 7:15: "Beware of false Prophets, who come to you in sheep's clothing, but inwardly are ravenous wolves".

Immorality has become part of the lifestyle of the world we are living in today. There is no fear of Elohiym in this generation. Everywhere you turn, all you can see is lawlessness! The conviction of sin in this generation has been totally ruled out. The fear of our LORD Jesus Christ is far gone. To make matters worse, some leaders in the body of Christ are recruiting new members into their sex rituals in order to sustain the power that brings crowd, fame and wealth. No wonder Jesus said judgement will start from His church (1 Peter 4:17).

Yahusha called them a brood of vipers! Matthew 12:34-35: Brood of vipers! How can you, being evil, speak good things? For out of the abundance of the heart the mouth speaks. A good man out of the good treasure of his heart brings forth good things, and an evil man out of the evil treasure brings forth evil things (Matthew 3:7). Today what is going on in most churches is worse than in the days of Sodom and Gomorrah. Everybody does whatever he or she wants and preaches whatever suits them, this is why the kingdom of darkness is prevailing over the lives of most believers.

## Image of the beast

Revelation 13:15 says: "And he had power to give life unto the image of the beast, that the image of the beast should both speak, and cause that as many as would not worship the image of the beast should be killed." (KJV)

Everything the Bible talks about that would happen in the end time is already happening under our own eyes. Some people have gone to the extent of creating an image and called it AI Jesus to minister to people. Is this what the word of God said we should do? AI has now taken the place of Jesus Christ to pray and minister to people to be saved! There is no fear of Elohiym again in this generation! Believers that are supposed to operate as kings and priests are being influenced by the evil powers of this age. The precious name of our LORD and God Jesus Christ is now used to name a demonic image created by man, an entity that doesn't carry the presence and wisdom of Elohiym is now ministering to people, and ignorant Christians are now bowing down to a talking image whose name is AI Jesus! This is insane! This is the highest height of blasphemy! It's a big shame that people that are supposed to defend their priesthood calling have turned it to a rag!

Matthew 24:4-5, Jesus speaks: "Take heed that no one deceives you. For many will come in My name, saying, 'I am the Christ,' and will deceive many.

Exodus 20:4-5a says: "You must not make any idol for yourself. Do not make a false god in the shape of anything that is in the sky above. Do not make one in the shape of anything on the earth or in the sea. You must not bend down your head to any idol or worship it. I am the LORD Your God and I want you to belong to Me alone. (EASY)

My advice to you is for you to repent and come back to your Maker quickly because no one can stand His wrath.

2 Chronicles 7:14 says: If My people who are called by My name will humble themselves, and pray and seek My face, and turn from their wicked ways, then I will hear from heaven, and will forgive their sin and heal their land.

If the body of Jesus Christ has to take over nations for Him, then we believers of Christ have to repent and be willing to carry our cross! Jesus warned the seven churches in Revelation 2:1-29 and Revelation 3:1-22, He is warning His church now to repent and come back to their priesthood which Christ called us to fulfil. He is the head of His church; anyone who wants to follow Him should be willing and obedient to carry their cross and keep to His ways. Until the body of Jesus Christ goes back to Elohiym and totally surrenders to His will, the body of Christ will still be oppressed by the powers of darkness. The day the body of Christ will come to operate in the fullness of God's power just as in the days of the Apostles in the book of Acts, it will be so powerful! And this is God's desire for all His children, to operate in the fullness of His power, because this is the only way to be His ambassadors and bring glory to His Holy name.

2 Corinthians 5:20 says: Now then, we are ambassadors for Christ, as though God were pleading through us: We implore you on Christ's behalf, be reconciled to God.

Elohiym the Most High God wants to pour out His Spirit upon His children according to Joel 2:28-30, but we have to be prepared because it's going to be so great. That means we have to strive in the spirit continuously till we see His glory poured out in this generation. Just imagine how this world would be if all believers come to know Him through His word and keep His commandments. There will be no room for any devil to operate! The reason the devil is oppressing the church is because the church of Christ is lacking love, wisdom, knowledge, understanding and discernment.

Daniel 1:20 says: Then the king interviewed them, and among them all none was found like Daniel, Hananiah, Mishael, and Azariah; therefore they served before the king. And in all matters of wisdom and understanding about which the king examined them, he found them ten times better than all the magicians and astrologers who were in all his realm.

If the church of Jesus Christ is operating in the place Christ has placed us, Satan wouldn't have had the opportunity to attack the children of God the way he is attacking now. We have to totally separate ourselves from all the works of darkness and become like a child to follow Him wherever He leads us to. If something is not done fast in this generation, the youths of this generation will completely forget God and perish! This is very serious; how can we be the light of the world and we have allowed darkness to take over our families, cities, and nations.

The church that is supposed to operate in the fear of the LORD God Almighty Elohiym, with wisdom and discernment, to discern all the works of darkness and pray against it and cancel them, are the ones inviting the devil to take over. Many ministers have gone against God's law of marriage, they are now being controlled by the same demonic spirit that was controlling the people of Sodom and Gomorrah! They have turned the Scriptures around to a way that soothes them! No regard for God's commandments.

The reason Daniel was ten times more intelligent than all the wizards that the king had, was because Daniel had made up his mind that he would not defile himself with the portion of the king's delicacies, nor with the wine which he drank, nor live a life of immorality. Daniel honoured Elohiym by depriving himself of the pleasures of the world that the king offered him. But now most believers have yielded themselves to the evil one who at the end will give them conditions on how to worship God the Father Yahuah Elohiym and our LORD and Saviour Yahusha Ha-Mashiach.

For us to see the former and latter rain in this generation, we must go back to our Maker in total repentance so that He can heal our land! Look at the rate of illnesses that's invading our nations, do you think this is a coincidence? Of course not! It is because the light has been put off, and evil powers have taken over the earth. Christians that are supposed to be watchmen, to discern and know that something is really wrong in the realm of the spirit, and wake up, take their position and pray and pray till they see changes, until God Elohiym sends His angels to come and shift things in the realm of the spirit, are busy chasing money and preaching another gospel. People are joining the occult because they want to make it big time! Selling their precious souls in exchange of wealth that they will die and leave, lack of wisdom and greed!

Mark 8:36 says: For what shall it profit a man, if he gains the whole world, and loses his soul?

There is no amount of wealth in this world that should ever make anyone sell his precious soul. You are created to reign on earth as king and priest, and now you want to be a slave to the devil! You go to sleep, and you don't have peace! Why? Because the devil cannot give you anything for free! So, it is left for you to be wise and obey God's commandments and live a peaceful life.

The Apostles of Jesus Christ became so powerful because they surrendered and laid down their lives at the feet of Jesus Christ to be used by Him. They were completely dead to the flesh! They were living a consecrated life, a life of prayer and fasting and going from place to place preaching the true gospel, with great persecution. They weren't busy buying expensive private jets, living in multimillion-dollar mansions, and boasting about it. We have to operate as kings and priests in our callings, because we all have a calling to fulfil. Whether as a leader, or as a teacher, or as a minister of the gospel, or as a politician or as banker, or as a businessman or woman, or as an author, or as a homemaker, or as a songwriter, or as a gospel singer, or as a lawyer, whatever your calling is, you are to operate under the priesthood of Christ, in order to bring changes in this generation.

## Time to surrender to Elohiym

We have spent so much time following the ways of the Gentiles! Now it is time for us to surrender totally to the Holy Spirit and for Him to mould and make us to be who He has created us to be. If the body of Yahusha wants to operate in the supernatural and restrain the powers of darkness, we must totally walk in complete obedience to God's commandments! The powers of darkness are advancing daily, and the body of Christ is sleeping. The problem with most believers is that they don't understand spiritual things! They are not aware that we are not fighting against flesh and blood but against principalities and powers that are operating in the spirit realms. The powers of darkness are working tirelessly continuously day and night to achieve their wicked agenda here on earth; they never give up! If the body of Christ understands how serious and wicked these demonic forces and the princes of darkness are, the body of Christ will wake up!

Let me tell you, going to church alone is not enough to operate in the power of the Holy Spirit and live a life of victory. Until you come to understand spiritual things, and begin to operate in that realm, you are still a baby! For God to speak to the Prophets in the Bible and empowered them to carry out His great plans, which they did; and for Him to transform the lives of the Apostles and do great things through them, this is to tell you that these men were totally obedient to God. These men did not play around! They were living a life of total consecration. That was the reason God Adonai used them to do supernatural things on this earth!

We have to be serious with this God that we are serving, if we want to do great things that eyes have not yet seen nor ears hath heard; this is the time for all believers to be watchful and be diligent in seeking the LORD God Almighty Elohiym because the coming of our LORD and Saviour Yahusha is at hand.

Revelation 16:15 says: "Behold, I am coming like a thief. Blessed is he who stays awake and who keeps his clothes (that is, stays spiritually ready for the LORD'S return), So that he will not be naked-spiritually unprepared-and men will not see his shame."

Apostle Paul wrote in 2 Thessalonians 2:5-8: "Don't you remember that when I was still with you, I used to tell you about this? And you know what currently restrains him, so that he will be revealed in his time. For the mystery of lawlessness is already at work, but the one now restraining will do so until he is out of the way, and then the lawless one will be revealed. The LORD Jesus will destroy him with the breath of His mouth and will bring him to nothing at the appearance of His coming."

Whether we like it or not, the darkness that is invading our cities, and nations of the world, is affecting every one of us, even the agents of Satan that are working for him are still suffering because they have been deceived by the devil! It is never too late to walk with the Holy Spirit. This is the only way we can stop the powers of darkness that are invading our nations. Once we surrender to God's authority, walking in line with His will and purpose; He will then raise a standard against the powers of darkness.

Amos 3:3 says: Can two walk together, except they are agreed?

John 14:13-14, Jesus said: However, when He, the Spirit of truth, has come, He will guide you into all truth; for He will not speak on His own authority, but whatever He hears He will speak; and He will tell you things to come. He will glorify Me, for He will take of what is Mine and declare it to you.

Moses walked with the Almighty God Yahuah and had several great encounters with the Holy Spirit and God did great signs and wonders through him, because he understood God and had a relationship with Him. The Apostles walked with God Elohiym and had great encounters with the Holy Spirit and the Holy Spirit did great miracles through them because they were totally obedient to Him. All the great Prophets, men and women that are recorded in the Bible, who did great things were all obedient to Him and they had great encounters with Yahuah Adonai and His angels. It is God that gives gifts to men, and He will only empower you with His gifts based on your faithfulness to His commandments (cf. 1 Corinthians 12:6-11).

Ephesians 4:7-8,11-14, Paul wrote: But to each one of us grace was given according to the measure of Christ's gifts. Therefore, He says: "When He ascended on high, He led captivity captive and gave gifts to men." And He Himself gave some to be Apostles, some Prophets, some evangelists, and some pastors and teachers; for the equipping of the saints, for the work of the ministry, for the edifying of the body of Christ, till we all come to the unity of the faith and of the knowledge of the Son of God, to a perfect man, to the measure of the stature of the fullness of Christ: that we should no longer be children, tossed to and fro and carried about with every wind of doctrine, by the trickery of men, in the cunning craftiness of deceitful plotting, but speaking the truth in love, may grow up in all things into Him who is the head-Christ.

Therefore, for your own good, refuse to remain a child in the kingdom of God! Aim to operate at the level the Holy Spirit wants you to operate; because you are in Christ, and those that are in Christ don't operate in the flesh, they operate in the spirit, because life is spiritual! And those that operate in the spirit are the ones in control of the things of God; these are the people that do not compromise with the devil. These are the ones that decree a thing and it comes to pass because the Almighty God honours their words; just as you feed and train your physical body to grow, likewise, train your spirit man to grow, in order to operate in the supernatural; because life is spiritual!

## Office of the priesthood

The office of the priesthood is a significant office that only serious believers who are ready to pay the price operate in; without the office of the priesthood, Christianity will be like every other religion. For you to become a son and be empowered by Elohiym to operate in the office of the priesthood, you must totally surrender to His will and allow the Holy Spirit to be your Master. Whatever He tells you to do, that's what you will do. Just as Mary the mother of Yahusha said to His disciples "whatever He says to you, do it." (John 2:5), this is when He will empower you to walk in the fruit of the Spirit, which is love, joy, peace, kindness, faithfulness, patience, goodness, gentleness and self-control (Galatians 5:22-23). Without these qualities, you cannot grow to operate under the priesthood of Christ; Apostle Paul wrote to the churches in Galatia in Galatians 4:1: Now I say that the heir, as long as he is a child, does not differ at all from a slave, though he is master of all, but is under guardians and stewards until the time appointed by the father.

This is the reason why many Christians are quoting Scriptures, and nothing is happening and they become so frustrated, and they start saying all sorts of things about God; I don't believe in the Bible anymore! I have been praying and nothing is happening. It is because they haven't crucified their flesh, they lack the fruit of the Spirit! They're still babies in the kingdom of God. The only way any believer can grow to become a son is living by the word of God and seeking the presence of the LORD God Almighty always, this is when you can grow in the spirit and become a son and operate as a king and priest. "If you don't cherish your office, there's no way the office will cherish you."

Hebrews 5:12-14 says: "For though this time you ought to be teachers, you need someone to teach you again the first principles of the oracles of God; And you have come to need milk and not solid food. For everyone who partakes only of milk is unskilled in the word of righteousness, for he is a babe. But solid food belongs to those who are full age, that is, those who by reason of use have their senses exercised to discern both good and evil."

In Ephesians 1:17-19, Apostle Paul prays for the church: That the God of our LORD Jesus Christ, the Father of glory, may give to you the spirit of wisdom and revelation in the knowledge of Him, the eyes of your understanding being enlightened; that you may know what is the hope of His calling, what are the riches of the glory of His inheritance in the saints, and what is the exceeding greatness of His power toward us who believe, according to the working of His mighty power.

Those that have come to the full knowledge of our LORD and Saviour Yahusha and are living for Him are the ones that are operating in the power of God. They have crucified their flesh and have surrendered totally to God; they have the revelation of Yahusha! The word of God has become part of them. These are the unshakable ones in the kingdom of God! The power of God Adonai is in you because the Holy Spirit is in you, and it is the Holy Spirit that will work through you to accomplish whatever He wants to accomplish in your life and through you. Until the word of God becomes so real to you, and be part of you, it will not benefit you, you have to see the word of God as Elohiym Himself speaking to you and living inside of you.

Ephesians 3:20 says: Now to Him who is able to do far more abundantly than all that we ask or think, according to the power at work within us.

## Sons and daughters to manifest Him

You are not born again to remain as a child but to grow to become the son of the Most High God; study the word of Yahuah and have full knowledge of His word so that you can be able to stand firm in the truth and defend it. The reason why most believers are being deceived by Satanic ministers is because they don't have full knowledge of the word of God. And that is why those preachers are getting away with the lies that they are preaching. Assuming all believers know the word of God, do you think these false preachers will still be preaching the gospel? Of course not! They would have repented or stopped preaching because no one would attend their meetings anymore.

When you are a baby in the kingdom of God, you will be weak in the spirit! Because your vessel is empty; if people who practised other religions who don't have the Holy Spirit in them, fast and pray several times a day to their god, how much more, followers of Yahusha who have the Holy Spirit? We are to pray continually without ceasing till we leave this earth (cf. 1 Thessalonians 5:17). This is the only way we can be sons and daughters of God and take care of our Father's business on earth and bring glory to His Holy name.

We have no excuse not to manifest His power and glory if we are praying and seeking His presence daily and studying His word. We are saying we want revival, but ask yourself this question; how can there be revival when the body of Christ is far from obeying the word of Yahusha? In churches, people hardly trust each other, people that are supposed to represent Christ are betraying one another, and we want to see revival. How?

2 Timothy 2:15 says: Be diligent to present yourself approved to God, a worker who does not need to be ashamed, rightly dividing the word of truth.

Many preachers will preach the Bible, but they are not living by it. They are deceiving themselves! Some people are claiming to be born again but they are more wicked than the devil. No one can mock God Almighty and get away with it! That is why Yahusha never honours the words they declare! The word of God is to guide us to all truth, we are to honour the word of Yahusha and embrace it so that Yahusha can honour

His word in our mouth; when you're full of the word of God, and walk by it, you will be full of the Holy Spirit. The Holy Spirit is on this earth to help us, but He can only help us to accomplish what we were called to accomplish when we put Him as the number one person in our life, and obey His commandments; that's when He will turn our lives around to bring glory and honour to the Holy name of Yahusha Ha-Mashiach.

John 16:13-14, Jesus says: However, when He, the Spirit of truth, has come, He will guide you into all truth; for He will not speak on His own authority, but whatever He hears He will speak; and He will tell you things to come. He will glorify Me, for He will take of what is Mine and declare it to you.

Psalm 119:105 says: Your word is a lamp to my feet and a light to my path.

In Romans 8:15, Paul wrote: The Spirit you received does not make you slaves, so that you live in fear again; rather, the Spirit you received brought about your adoption to sonship. And by Him we cry "Abba Father."

When you continue to obey God's word and you allow Him to guide you, that is when you will grow in the spirit realm and be empowered to operate as sons and daughters of the Most High God and live a life of constant victory. And as a son, as you continue to seek the face of God in prayers and in fasting always, doing the work of evangelism, living by the true word of God, Elohiym will then increase your ranking in the office of the priesthood; because everything in the supernatural realm is based on ranking.

Matthew 16:19 says: "And I will give you the keys of the kingdom of heaven, and whatever you bind on earth will be bound in heaven, and whatever you loose on earth will be loosed in heaven, (cf. Job 22:28).

God Almighty Elohiym created us and has put His Spirit in us so that we can represent Him on earth, which is carrying out His plans on this earth and making sure they stand firm; but as a child in the kingdom, you won't be able to operate in the power of the Holy Spirit, in order to execute God's plan and to see that it stands. So, this is why God wants all His children to grow in the spirit; and until you grow in the spirit and take authority over the kingdom of darkness, you will remain a victim to the devil! For the powers of darkness to surrender to the words you declare, you must be an obedient child of God and be fed constantly with the true word of God!

This is the reason the Holy Spirit gave gifts to some to be Apostles, some Prophets, some Evangelists, some Pastors and Teachers to equip and build up the body of Christ; so that everyone would come to the full knowledge of Christ and operate as sons and daughters of Adonai. So, as a leader in Christ, God has ordained you to lead and build up His children to maturity in the full knowledge of Him so that they can walk obediently in God's word fulfilling their purpose.

Matthew 7:13-14 says: "Enter by the narrow gate; for wide is the gate and broad is the way that leads to destruction, and there are many who go in by it. Because narrow is the gate and difficult is the way which leads to life, and there are few who find it.

There are so many believers today all over the world, but the Bible tells us that only few have found the truth and are walking by it; because the majority of the children of the Most High God are spiritually blind, and are being deceived by the evil ones. It is the knowledge and revelation of the word of God that you know that would grant you access to walk in the fullness of God. This is why many believers are under the influence of demonic powers, and they can't perceive it; when you are under demonic influence and your spirit man is not reacting against it, then something is really wrong with you. That means your spirit man is weak and is sleeping in the spirit realm.

As a child of Elohiym, when you see something that is not of God, you are supposed to know because the Holy Spirit will quicken your spirit and make you aware of what is going on. There's no way you can be deceived when your spirit man is active in the spirit realm, when you are walking with the Holy Spirit obediently. This is the main reason why God wants His children to grow in the knowledge of Him and operate in the gift of discernment so that we will not fall a victim to these demonic powers. When you see some of the preachers that are under demonic anointing, you will know because of the things they preach and what they do. These people are wolves in sheep's clothing (cf. Matthew 7:15).

And that is the more reason the few that have known the truth should not stop praying for God to intervene and bring His children out from every influence of demonic powers.

If not for the mercies of God Yahusha towards me, I would have died long ago, because I was a victim to these false ministers, because I refused to study the word of God and to know Him personally so that I can walk and operate in the truth and fulfil what He has called me to do.

2 Corinthians 11:13-15 says: For such are false Apostles, deceitful workers, transforming themselves into Apostles of Christ. And no wonder! For Satan himself transforms himself into an angel of light. Therefore, it is no great thing if his ministers also transform themselves into ministers of righteousness, whose end will be according to their works.

Hosea 4:6, God speaks: My people are destroyed for lack of knowledge; because thou hast rejected knowledge, I will also reject thee, that thou shalt be no priest to me: seeing thou hast forgotten the law of thy God, I will also forget thy children.

Adonai, the Creator of the universe expects all believers to continue to pray ceaselessly because He knows the enemies are everywhere looking for whom to destroy. We are to be like Christ our High Priest;

when Christ was on this earth, He always excluded Himself and went to a quiet place and prayed; prayer was the greatest part of His ministry! And that was why His ministry made a great impact on this earth and is still making and changing lives.

The Almighty Elohiym has called us out of darkness and brought us into His kingdom to be His priests and to rule as kings here on earth and bring changes to this generation. So, the church has to strive in the place of prayer just as the Apostles; they prayed and prayed till the Holy Spirit came down and empowered them, before they went out and started their ministries. So, let's continue to strive in prayers till we see the mighty hand of God upon our lives and in the lives of our loved ones and the entire world. When you look at yourself in the mirror, what you see reflects what you look like. Likewise, our life is to reflect Christ to the world! And not the other way round.

2 Corinthians 3:18 says: But we all, with open face beholding as in a glass the glory of the LORD God, are changed into the same image from glory to glory, even as by the Spirit of the LORD God.

This is God's wish for all His children, to go from glory to glory, in the kingdom of God. That is how our rank in the spirit realm will also increase! As believers, for us to operate under the priesthood of Christ, there are qualities we must acquire to be approved by God for Him to empower us to operate as sons and daughters, kings and priests in the priesthood office.

1 Thessalonians 2:4, Apostle Paul speaks: "But as we have been approved by God to be entrusted with the gospel, even so we speak, not as pleasing men, but God who tests our hearts." (NKJV)

## Qualities we must attain to operate in the office of the priesthood

1. **Purity**: Purity is one of the greatest qualities every follower of Yahusha should acquire! Before God Yahusha can ordain anyone to operate in the office of the priesthood, that person must walk in purity. Purity is what allows us to dwell in the presence of God. For us to operate as sons and daughters of the most high God, we must make sure we are walking in a way that is pleasing to God and not pleasing to man. Our garment must be clean for us to function effectively under the priesthood of Christ.

Colossians 3:5 says: Put to death, therefore, whatever belongs to your earthly nature; sexual immorality, impurity, lust, evil desires and greed, which is idolatry.

We must walk in complete holiness, without blemish or fault; we must have a pure heart before we can carry His presence and operate in the office of the priesthood! Anything less than this is unacceptable to the Holy and perfect God.

2. **Humility**: Humility is what qualifies us to operate as sons and daughters of the Most High God Adonai. We must be humble before God and man. Our humility is what attracts God's favour upon our lives. Before Elohiym can use us to represent Him here on earth and be a blessing to our generations, we must be completely humble. This is a fundamental principle that should be seen in the lives of every believer in Christ. Jesus is our number one example; He was completely humble and obedient before God and man. So, if we want to operate as sons and daughters of the Most High God, then we must humble ourselves under the leadership of the Holy Spirit for Him to guide us to do His will. Yahusha humbled Himself to come to this earth as a human and died as a criminal to save humanity from eternal death.

1 Peter 5:6 says: "Therefore humble yourselves under the mighty hand of God, that He may exalt you in due time.

Luke 14:11, Jesus said: "For whoever exalts himself will be humbled, and whoever humbles himself will be exalted."

Proverbs 16:5 says: Everyone who is proud and arrogant in heart is disgusting and exceedingly offensive to the LORD; Be assured he will not go unpunished. (AMP)

James 4:6: says: "But He gives more grace. Therefore, He says, 'God resists the proud, but gives grace to the humble.'"

3. **Burden Bearer**: For us to be empowered by Elohiym Yahusha and operate as sons and daughters in the priesthood office, we must lay down our own burdens and make God's burdens our burden. Moses was a man after God's heart, he knew how much God loved His people and he laid aside his desires and pursued God's desires, and the Most High God Elohiym empowered him to deliver the whole nation of Israel. The reason why so many ministers opened churches is not because they love God and want to see souls saved; it's because of their personal gain, and that is why they don't care about leading God's people in the right direction. Just take a close look at what is going on in most churches, you will see the height of wickedness, you can see that these people are not burden bearers. It's all about them and not Christ!

Hebrews 11:24-26 says: By faith Moses, when he became of age, refused to be called the son of Pharaoh's daughter, choosing rather to suffer affliction with the people of God than to enjoy the passing pleasures of sin, esteeming the reproach of Christ greater riches than the treasures in Egypt; for he looked to the reward.

Until we make God's burdens our burdens, which is soul winning, praying for the lost souls, doing evangelism, preaching the true gospel of Jesus Christ that will lead people to Christ and abide by His word, so that they can fulfil God's plan and purpose for their lives, He cannot empower us to operate in the office of the priesthood. The disciples of Jesus Christ had to abandon their fishing business and follow Jesus Christ to win souls. And they all preached the true gospel; making disciples for Christ and none of them were after their own gain. So, we must walk faithfully with Him, if we want to prevail over the kingdom of darkness.

4. **Stamina to pray and fast**: For any believer to grow in the realm of the spirit and operate under the priesthood of Christ, that person must have stamina to pray and fast as often as the Holy Spirit leads him or her. In Acts 1:12-14, before Jesus ascended to heaven, the disciples of Jesus were asked by Him to remain in Jerusalem praying until they were baptised with the Holy Spirit, to be empowered first before they can become His witnesses; because Jesus knew that they will face lots of temptations and trials. So, the disciples waited in Jerusalem praying in the upper room until they were baptised in the Holy Spirit; the Scriptures said, they began to speak in different kinds of tongues, people's languages, because everyone that was present that day heard them in their own language and more than 3,000 people gave their lives to Christ (Acts 2:1-41).

Jesus Christ Himself before He started His ministry, the Scripture says, the Holy Spirit led Him to the wilderness to be tempted by the devil; and for forty days and forty nights; He was without food and water;

He was praying and fasting seeking the face of the Father Yahuah (Matthew 4:1-11). Moses was another example, who through prayers and fasting carried out the will of God. The Bible said, Moses was on Mount Sinai, praying for forty days and forty nights with no food and water, in the presence of God, being empowered by the Holy Spirit, receiving instructions from Him (cf. Exodus 34:28-35). So, for any believer to operate as a son or daughter of the Most High God in the supernatural, that person must have the stamina to pray and fast at all times and wait upon Adonai.

Luke 6:12 says: "Now it came to pass in those days that He went out to the mountain to pray and continued all night in prayer to God."

The reason why many believers struggle in life and are being oppressed by the enemies is because they don't know how to wait on the LORD God Almighty in prayers and in fasting. There are times Elohiym wants you to remain in His presence in prayer and in fasting till you see things shift in the spirit realm; because life is spiritual, everything that happens on this earth is being controlled in the spirit realm, so, we must always be vigilant in prayers and fasting to make sure we are in sync with the Holy Spirit in fulfilling our assignments. Don't be a sleepy Christian! Build your spiritual strength through prayers and fasting and learn how to wait upon the LORD God Elohiym till He empowers you and gives you instructions on what to do in order to fulfil destiny.

Many people because of impatience went ahead of God Yahusha and that was the end of their story. Many ministers open churches without waiting upon the LORD God Almighty in prayer and in fasting to hear what He will say, and they end up selling their souls to the devil. They don't know that it is in the place of waiting upon the LORD Yahusha that they will be empowered and receive instructions on what to do to fulfil purpose.

Many children of God are going about looking for a minister to lay hands on them, and that is how the ministers would transfer demonic spirits to them; when they are supposed to lay their hands on themselves if they know who they are in Christ. Christ came and showed us examples by praying and fasting all throughout His ministry, so that we can do the same and operate as sons and daughters of the Most High God. No one can go far in this kingdom if that person does not have the stamina to pray and fast.

Isaiah 40:31 wrote: But those who wait on the LORD God shall renew their strength; they shall mount up with wings like eagles, they shall run and not be weary, they shall walk and not faint.

Without being trained by the Holy Spirit, you cannot last in the ministry, and in the kingdom of God Elohiym, because temptations and trials will definitely come, and you can never stand it; that is why many have fallen into the lion's den and they are unable to come out.

Ephesians 6:10-11 says: Finally, my brethren, be strong in the LORD God and in the power of His might. Put on the whole armour of God, that you may be able to stand against the wiles of the devil.

5. **Discernments**: The gift of discernment is one of the most important gifts all believers should have; without the gift of discernment, it will be impossible for us to operate as sons and daughters in the office of the priesthood. The reason believers are making a lot of mistakes, falling into the hands of the devil is because they don't have the gift of discernment. Without this gift, you cannot function effectively in the kingdom of God! If Jesus Christ, the Prophets, and the Apostles did not operate in the gifts of discernment, do you think their ministries would've made any impact? The reason their ministries made great impact is because of the high level of discernment they operated at.

This is the reason God made these gifts available for us so that we can be empowered in order to fulfil our assignments on earth. So, it is very vital that every child of Elohiym operates in this gift. Jesus Christ knew everyone's thoughts when He was on this earth, and He knew everything that was happening and would happen! That was why He was different from all the Prophets who had come and gone. In Acts 16:16-19, we read how Paul and Silas, on their way to pray, met a certain slave girl who was possessed with a spirit of divination, and used to bring her master much profit by fortune-telling. This girl followed them for many days saying, "These men are the servants of the Most High God, who proclaim to us the way of salvation."

But Paul after a few days discerned it and was very angry and commanded the spirit to come out of her in the name of our LORD God Yahusha. Assuming he didn't have the spirit of discernment, the girl would have accomplished her assignments, she was telling the truth but with the spirit of divination. She wanted people to assume that she was a true servant of God, and that she was with the Apostles, so that the people will continue to patronise her; but thank God Paul was so smart to discern it, and he cast out the devil from her.

Many Christians claim to be filled with the Holy Spirit, but they are actually operating under the spirit of divination, which is witchcraft. Their mission is to deceive and destroy the children of God so that they would not fulfil their purpose! They will pretend as if they're born again, they will speak in tongues, call the name of Jesus, but they are vipers!

That is why Elohiym wants every believer to operate in the gift of discernment. Assuming everyone is operating in the gift of discernment, do you think the enemies will be able to attack the church the way they are doing now? Until the church gets to that place of the priesthood, where everyone is operating in the gift of discernment, the body of Christ will still be operating in the flesh and be oppressed by the powers of darkness.

Hebrews 5:14 says: But solid food is for the mature, for those who have their powers of discernment trained by constant practice to distinguish good from evil.

Philippians 1:9-10 says: "And this I pray, that your love may abound still more and more in knowledge and all discernment, that you may approve the things that are excellent, that you may be sincere and without offence till the day of Christ.

Imagine the body of Christ operating at this level, do you think Satan's kingdom will advance and invade the earth as it is now? Of course not, it will be impossible! So, we need to wake up from our sleep and say, enough is enough, and take back our authority in Christ and begin to operate in the manifold gifts of the Spirit.

In Romans 13:11, Apostle Paul wrote: Beside this you know the time, that the hour has come for you to wake from sleep. For salvation is nearer to us now than when we first believed. Christ is coming back soon, and He is not coming for a church that has stains or wrinkles, (cf. Ephesians 5:27).

6. **Faithfulness**: Elohiym the Most High God wants us to be faithful to His commandments at all times; our faithfulness means steadfast loyalty to His commandments! It is our faithfulness that enables us to grow in the spirit and operate as kings and priests. Apostle Paul says in his letter in 1 Thessalonians 2:11-

12, "As you know how we exhorted, and comforted, and charged every one of you, as a father does his own children, that you would walk worthy of God who calls you into His own kingdom and glory."

Luke 12:42-44: And the Lord said, "Who then is that faithful and wise steward, whom his master will make ruler over his household, to give them their portion of food in due season? Blessed is that servant whom his master will find so doing when he comes. Truly, I say to you that he will make him ruler over all that he has.

We must be faithful followers of Jesus Christ at all times! That means following His commandments even when it seems so hard to abide by it. Honouring and obeying Elohiym in every aspect of our life is what empower us to operate in the priesthood and overcome all the powers of darkness! The authority and the power to operate in the supernatural can only be invested in us when we honour His word by keeping His commandments. The Apostles were so faithful to Yahusha, they walked with Him in meekness and honesty and God did great miracles through them. So, for us to see the mighty power of God in our lives and through us, we must walk faithfully in keeping His commandments.

Proverbs 28:20b says: A faithful man will abound with blessings.

**7. Love:** Elohiym the Most High God is love, and whoever abides in Him operates in love! So, for any believer to function and operate as a son or daughter of the Most High God, that person must operate in love; Without love no one can be able to please God and be empowered to do great things in God's kingdom. Love is the only thing that would compel you to intercede for others, to give to others, not to talk down on others, and to win souls for the kingdom of Christ. Love is the only thing that would make you obey the voice of Yahuah when He instructs you to do something that is out of your will. If Yahuah didn't show His love to us, we all would've perished a long time ago. Our love for Him and others should be unconditional because His love towards us is an unconditional love. His love for us should inspire us to love people with compassion even when they don't deserve it. And love covers a multitude of sins! So, it is one of the greatest commandments that we should follow.

John 15:12-13 says: This is My commandment, that you love one another as I have loved you. Greater love has no one than this, than to lay down one's life for his friends.

1 John 4:16 says: And we have known and believed the love that God has for us. God is love, and he who abides in love abides in God, and God in him.

# The office of an intercessor in the priesthood

Romans 8:26-27 says: Likewise, the Spirit also helps in our weaknesses. For we do not know what we should pray for as we ought, but the Spirit Himself makes intercession for us with groanings which cannot be uttered. Now He who searches the hearts knows what the mind of the Spirit is, because He makes intercession for the saints according to the will of God.

The Holy Spirit is constantly making intercession for us with groanings which cannot be uttered. The reason we are standing strong each day and still striving to do what God Almighty has assigned us to do, is because our intercessor the Holy Spirit is interceding for us daily. So, as believers we are called to do the same! Every believer is called to be an intercessor, to stand in the gap for others, for God's divine purpose to manifest in the lives of our loved ones and in the world. The first intercessor is our LORD Jesus Christ, who came and died for us. This is a very significant office; without an intercessor, a lot of people will perish; and for the will of God to be done on this earth. We need intercessors that would bring the supernatural power of God's kingdom to manifest in the natural.

1 Timothy 2:1 says: "Therefore I exhort first of all that supplications, prayers, intercessions, and giving of thanks be made for all men." (NKJV)

The reason the kingdom of darkness is advancing is because there are not enough intercessors! Based on the number of believers all over the world, if there were great numbers of intercessors in the world today, this world wouldn't be the way it is now. Many people are called to be intercessors but because they are not ready to carry their cross, they are unable to fulfil their assignment as intercessors. And also, most intercessors have fallen into the hands of false ministers of the gospel, and their gifts have been stolen from them. No intercessor who is still operating in the flesh can carry God's presence and operate in His power. As an intercessor, you must walk in the fruit of the Spirit for the Holy Spirit to empower you to stand in the gap for others.

There are three levels of intercession: There is the priestly, the prophetic, and the kingly. Our LORD Yahusha operated in all the levels of the priesthood! The priestly intercessors are those who stand in the gap between Elohiym and man! Praying for God's mercies to prevail in the lives of people and praying for souls to be won. God is looking for people that would operate in the Melchizedek order! We don't have enough time left! The kingdom of darkness is increasing daily; and the body of Christ is sleeping; the return of Yahusha is very close, this is the time to avoid every distraction and focus only on Christ and the assignments He has given to each one of us. We are to stand pure before God to intercede for the dying souls; this is our priesthood calling! I pray God opens your spiritual eyes to see the countless souls that're locked up in the realm of darkness, so that you will wake up and intercede for the lost souls.

The prophetic priests are the watchmen of God's people! These are the ones God Almighty has anointed to see into the realm of the spirit and carry out His plans and bring it to fulfilment. These are watchmen who have been assigned to stop the works of darkness and bring judgment to the powers of darkness. Abraham, Moses, Elisha, Elijah, Ezekiel and the Apostles all operated in this priesthood. I am aware that not everyone is called to be a prophet, but God has called us to be part of the prophetic priesthood generation. So, as we partner with the Holy Spirit; He will empower us to operate in the prophetic realm and bring complete judgment to the forces of darkness that are invading the earth and are influencing people to rebel against the will and purpose of God's plans for their lives.

Acts 2:17 says: "And it shall come to pass in the last days, says God, That I will pour out of My spirit on all flesh; Your sons and your daughters shall prophesy, your young men shall see visions, your old men shall dream dreams.

The kingly priesthood: God Almighty Elohiym wants us to rule and reign on this earth with authority as kings! Yahusha is the King of kings and the LORD of Lords. He has forever defeated Satan and all his powers and has made us kings to rule and reign here on earth! According to Matthew 18:18 that says: "Whatever we bind on earth is bound in heaven, and whatever we loose on earth will be loosed in heaven." The kingly priesthood office is for all believers to operate in the authority of Christ as king over all the powers of darkness; as an ambassador of Yahusha Ha-Mashiach, we are to operate as legislators and litigators here on earth; so, it is the level of your understanding of who you are in Christ that would determine the level in which you will operate at as kings. This is why it is vital for us to walk obediently with God so that He can impact us with supernatural knowledge of His words to enable us rule as kings on this earth.

When you see the lives of the Apostles, you can see the high level of grace they all had. They all fulfilled their priesthood ministries, because they walk faithfully with God. It is your level of knowledge of the word of God and the level of participation with the Holy Spirit that would determine the level of grace He will grant you. If there is someone who is praying for souls faithfully, abiding by the word of God, using his or her talent for the works of God, and there is another that just prays now and then, not interested in soul winning, not engaging with the Holy Spirit, not abiding by the commandments of the LORD God Almighty Elohiym, both of them cannot carry the same grace of the anointing. It doesn't matter how long you've been a believer, or the titles you give yourself; a believer that just gave his or her life to Christ newly and is walking faithfully with the Holy Spirit can carry more fire than you in the spirit realm.

## God's expectation

Hebrews 1:7: And of the angels He says, "Who makes His angels spirits and His ministers a flame of fire."

God expects every one of His children to be a flame of fire, because we are living in a world full of wickedness! Therefore, the only way we can live a life of constant victory and execute His plans in this wicked world is to be filled with the Holy Spirit. This is when we can become a terror to the kingdom of darkness. Look at the Apostles in the Bible, they were all flames of fire against the works of darkness, because they were totally obedient to Yahuah's commandments. They carried His presence wherever they went; they weren't after any wealth! They didn't compromise their priesthood calling. They counted it all joy even when they were beaten and put to prison for the sake of the gospel. Imagine people bringing in the sick to the street and laying them on beds so that the shadow of Peter can heal them (Acts 5:15-16). If Moses' heart was not after God's people, do you think God would've sent him to deliver His people? The reason God sent Moses was because He saw that his heart was after His people, the Israelites.

Hebrews 11:24-26 says: By faith Moses, when he became of age, refused to be called the son of Pharaoh's daughter, choosing rather to suffer affliction with the people of God than to enjoy the passing pleasures of sin, esteeming the reproach of

Christ greater riches than the treasures in Egypt; for he looked to the reward.

As a leader you must be faithful to His commandments and demonstrate God's love to others at all times for God to entrust you with His people. You don't just wake up, open a church, and give yourself a title: 'I am a Bishop, I am an Apostle, I am a Prophet, I am a Pastor.' You must earn it; it must be approved by God! For the number of Bishops, Apostles, Prophets and Pastors that are in the world today, the immoralities on this earth should have reduced, rather they are getting worse as days go by.

So many people are scared to go to church, why? Because of all the evil things they're seeing and hearing in most churches. Some new believers have gone back to the world because of the bad experiences they've had in the church. All these have to stop because the anger of the LORD God Almighty Elohiym is about to be released on those people who are using His Holy name to do evil.

Jeremiah 23:1-2 says: "Woe to the shepherds who destroy and scatter the sheep of My pasture!" says the LORD. Therefore, thus says the LORD God of Israel against the shepherds who feed My people: "You have scattered My flock, driven them away, and not attended to them. Behold, I will attend to you for the evil of your doings," says the LORD.

As sons and daughters of the Most high God Elohiym, we are God's ambassadors, we are to operate as a legislator and litigator. Every ambassador has laid down rules in the embassy of that nation for everyone who wants a visa to follow; and the rules stand until a new ambassador comes in and brings in his own new rules and cancels the existing one! Likewise, every son and daughter of God is to act as a legislator and a litigator; a legislator is someone who makes law; while a litigator is someone who helps someone take legal action. God wants us to operate as legislators and litigators, so that we can terminate every existing demonic law and establish His laws and make sure it stands firm on this earth.

Because of the faithfulness of Daniel, God demonstrated His power while Daniel was in the lion's den that the lion's became his friend instead of eating him up; this is what compelled king Darius to make a decree in the whole nation that everyone in his kingdom must worship the God of Daniel.

The reason why the body of Christ is being attacked today is because there are not many intercessors and watchmen that would change the existing satanic system of a place and decree the law of Christ to be established! Where the priesthood of Christ is in place, the church of Christ will prevail. The integrity of the church today is almost gone, because believers have left their priesthood office, and are busy doing things that are for their own gain.

For us to be able to terminate any existing Satanic law in a place or in a system and establish the law of

Yahuah, we must go back to our maker, repent and keep His commandments; our spiritual garments must be clean! We cannot operate as kings and priests if our spiritual garments have stains. Our spiritual garments must be pure before the LORD God Almighty Elohiym for us to operate in the supernatural; and for Satan not to hold anything against us!

Prophet Zechariah saw a vision, Joshua the high priest was putting on a very filthy garment which had prevented him from standing before the LORD God Almighty; and Satan standing at his right hand trying to oppose him from God's presence. God had to intervene and rebuke Satan and remove the filthy garment which Joshua was wearing and put a clean garment on him. The reason why so many ministers decree a thing and it doesn't come to pass is because they are not following God's way; God can only demonstrate His power when we are keeping His laws. Elohiym is a God of principles, He Himself keeps to His own words; so, how do you think you can disobey His words and still operate in His power? He is a Holy God! So, we must always be conscious of His presence not to grieve Him.

Zachariah 3:1-5: Then he showed me Joshua the high priest standing before the angel of the LORD, and Satan standing at his right hand to oppose him. And the Lord said to Satan, "The Lord who has chosen Jerusalem rebukes you! Is this not a brand plucked from the fire?" Now Joshua was clothed with filthy garments and was standing before the Angel. Then He answered and spoke to those who stood before Him, saying, "Take away the filthy garments from him." And to him He said, "See, I have removed your iniquity from you, and I will clothe you with rich robes." And I said, "Let them put a clean turban on his head." So, they put a clean turban on his head, and they put the clothes on him. And the angel of the Lord God stood by.

In Acts 19:14-17, we read about the seven sons of Sceva trying to cast out demons; these men saw how Apostle Paul was healing the sicks and casting out demons, they decided to do the same, and the evil spirit answered and said, "Jesus I know, and Paul I know but who are you?" and the man who had been possessed by the evil spirit leaped on them, overpowered them, and prevailed against them, and the seven sons fled out of the house naked and wounded. When we are living a life of immorality, we become filthy in the realm of the spirit, and become slaves to the devil, and that is when he becomes the boss, because it is only through sin and ignorance we can lose our birthright as sons and daughters of the Most High God. This is why God wants us to live holy! We can only defeat the kingdom of darkness and represent Him on earth when we are living holy, when we totally surrender to His will and walk with Him faithfully.

2 Peter 2:20-22, Peter wrote: For if, after they have escaped the pollution of the world through the

knowledge of the Lord and Saviour Jesus Christ, they are again entangled in them and overcome, the latter end is worse for them than the beginning. For it would have been better for them not to have known the way of righteousness, than having known it, to turn from the Holy commandment delivered to them. But it has happened to them according to the true proverb; "A dog returns to his own vomit," and "a sow, having washed, to her wallowing in the mire."

## Be focused on your assignments

As sons and daughters of the Most High God Elohiym, we should bear it in mind that our goal is Heaven. Elohiym Yahusha has a mandate for every one of us, and we are to work on His mandate; our time here on earth should be spent fulfilling His plans and purposes for our lives; that would constantly bring glory and honour to His Holy name. That means we need to engage in partnering with the Holy Spirit so that He can reveal to us what we have to do and how to fulfil it according to His time frame for our lives. We should remember that we are strangers on this earth, our home is heaven; we are here to start and finish what we were created for. A wise man will not live on this earth as if this earth is the final destination, you should live your life always prepared to meet with our LORD Yahusha when you leave this earth! Abraham understood this and he walked faithfully with God.

Hebrews 11:10 says: Abraham was confidently looking to the city with eternal foundations, a city designed and built by God.

Isaiah 62:6-7 says: "I have set watchmen on your walls, O Jerusalem; They shall never hold their peace, day or night. You who make mention of the LORD, do not keep silent, and give Him no rest till He establishes and till He makes Jerusalem a praise in the earth."

Day and night, every son and daughter of the Most High God is to intercede in prayers till the glory of God Elohiym manifests in all our cities and nations; until there is revival in every city! As intercessors, watchmen, or as gatekeepers, our assignment is to make sure no wolves get hold of God's people to snatch them away from the truth and their destiny. As kings and priests, we are to make sure the commandments of God stand; we are not here on earth to accept the utterances of the evil ones, we are here to uproot them out and let only the word of God stand.

We read how Elijah decreed and said to Ahab that there would be no rain and Elohiym honoured Elijah's words and rain ceased in that land for three years and he decreed again for rain to fall, and God honoured his words and brought rain on the land (1 Kings 17:1 ; cf. 1 Kings 18:1). So, wake up and begin to take possession of all what the enemies have taken from you, the time is short, it is time to rule as king and priest and manifest His glory; the world is getting darker and darker, we are to arise and shine our light so that people can come out of darkness and come into the marvellous light of Yahusha Elohiym.

Job 22:28 says: Thou shalt also decree a thing, and it shall be established unto thee; and the light shall shine upon thy ways. (KJV)

## Paul warns the church

In Acts 20:28-32, Apostle Paul wrote: "Therefore take heed to yourselves and to all the flock, among which the Holy Spirit has made you overseers, to shepherd the church of God which He purchased with His own blood. For I know this, that after my departure, savage wolves will come in among you, not sparing the flock. Also, from among yourselves men will rise up, speaking perverse things, to draw away the disciples after themselves. Therefore, watch and remember that for three years I did not cease to warn everyone night and day with tears. "So now, brethren, I commend you to God and to the word of His grace, which is able to build you up and give you an inheritance among all those who are sanctified."

When Apostle Paul was about to depart to Jerusalem, he called the elders of the church and instructed them to watch over the brethren, whom he was watching over, but now that he had to depart from them and might not return back, because of what the

Holy Spirit had revealed to him. He pleaded with the elders to do the same! This is the type of watchmen God is looking for, not church leaders that are misleading God's people to hell.

When God sees your faithfulness towards Him by watching over the few people He has entrusted to you, He gives you a larger congregation; from there, He will then give you a city, and then a nation, just as He gave the nation of Israel to Moses to deliver them from the land of Egypt. So, we have to persevere till we accomplish all that God has assigned for us to do. Whatever assignment our LORD Jesus Christ has given to you and I, we have to do it faithfully, watch and pray continually for the church which is Christ's body.

Apostle Paul speaking in 2 Thessalonians 1:11-12: "Therefore we also pray always for you that our God would count you worthy of His calling, and fulfil all the good pleasure of His goodness and the work of faith with power, that the name of our LORD Jesus Christ may be glorified in you, and you in Him, according to the grace of our God and the LORD Jesus Christ."

The Almighty God Elohiym is still looking for intercessors that would stand in the gap for this dying generation, people that have refused to bow down to Baal, people with integrity! People like Abraham, that God had to inform first about His plans to destroy Sodom and Gomorrah, and Abraham stood in the gap for his nephew Lot. God is still looking for people like Moses that stood for the children of Israel when God wanted to destroy them! God is still looking for people like Esther who went against the king's law by risking her own life in order to save her people, the Jews, from being killed by Haman. God is still looking for people like Daniel that interceded for his people continually till his prayers were answered! Like the Apostles who went through persecution to make sure the gospel is preached to everyone, and souls be won to Christ.

Ezekiel 22:30-31, God speaks: "So I sought for a man among them who would make a wall and stand in the gap before Me on behalf of the land, that I should not destroy it; but I found no one." "Therefore, I have poured out My indignation on them; I have consumed them with the fire of My wrath; and I have recompensed their deeds on their own heads," says the LORD God."

## The scattering horns

Zachariah 1:18 wrote: Then I raised my eyes and looked, and there were four horns. And I said to the angel who talked with me, "What are these?" So, he answered me, "These are the horns that have scattered Judah, Israel, and Jerusalem." Then the LORD God showed me four craftsmen. And I said, "What are these coming to do?" So, He said, "These are the horns that scattered Judah, so that no one could lift up his head; but the craftsmen are coming to terrify them, to cast out the horns of the nations that lifted up their horn against the land of Judah to scatter it."

These horns are principalities assigned to nations, to cities, to the church of Jesus Christ, to destroy and to make sure there are no believers that will operate as kings and priests. The duties of these high-ranking demons are to keep the people of God, a city or a nation, in total darkness, so that there would be no revival, and no one would be able to do great and mighty things for the kingdom of God. When you see a church where the people are keeping God's commandments, you will see the glory of God manifesting; and Satan will fight so hard to attack the people, and the more he comes against God's people, the more God empowers them to prevail over the powers of darkness.

So it is the assignment of the sons, the watchmen, intercessors, the gatekeepers, the seers, to live a life of holiness, watch and pray constantly and make sure the enemies are restrained from operating till the appointed time, when Christ will come for His church and put an end to Satan and his kingdom (2 Thessalonians 2:5-8); (cf. Revelation 20:10).

Ezekiel 3:16-21: "Now it came to pass at the end of seven days that the word of the Lord came to me, saying, "Son of man, I have made you a watchman for the house of Israel; therefore hear a word from My mouth, and give them warning from Me: When I say to the wicked, 'You shall surely die,' and you give him no warning, nor speak to warn the wicked from his wicked way, to save his life, that same wicked man shall die in his iniquity; but his blood I will require at your hand. Yet, if you warn the wicked, and he does not turn from his wickedness, nor from his wicked way, he shall die in his iniquity; but you have delivered your soul. "Again, when a righteous man turns from his righteousness and commits iniquity, and I lay a stumbling block before him, he shall die; because you did not give him warning, he shall die in his sin, and his righteousness which he has done shall not be remembered; but his blood I will require at your hand. Nevertheless, if you warn the righteous man that the righteous should not sin, and he does not sin, he shall surely live because he took warning; also, you will have delivered your soul."

The reason we shouldn't close our mouth from preaching the true gospel to the world is because we will be held responsible as believers; that is why Yahusha came to die for the whole world, and preached the gospel to His people and raised disciples and instructed them to do the same so that no one will have any excuse to give on that day of judgement; We are born again because someone preached the gospel to us, so it is now our duty to preach the truth to the people in the world! When you see preachers leading their members to hell, it is because they are of the devil. A true minister of Christ will only preach the true gospel of Yahusha, which is His birth, death and resurrection and not prosperity. This is how people can repent and come back to God in total obedience.

Apostle Paul wrote in Philippians 3:17-19: Brothers, join in imitating me, and keep your eyes on those who walk according to the example you have in us. For many, of whom I have often told you and now tell you even with tears, that they are the enemies of the cross of Christ; whose end is destruction, their god is their belly, and their glory is in their shame, who set their mind on earthly things. But our citizenship is in heaven, and from it we await a Saviour, the Lord Jesus Christ, who will transform our lowly body to be like His glorious body, by the power that enables Him even to subject all things to Himself.

As believers, we all have a role to play in order to fulfil the plans and purposes of God on this earth. If we do not do what we are called to do, then we have failed Yahuah Elohiym. We are to follow the footsteps of our LORD Adonai and the great men and women in the Bible and do what they did for the kingdom of Christ; the Apostles of Jesus Christ followed the steps of Jesus, they followed the steps of the Prophets of God, they carried their cross even unto death, they never compromised, they lived for Christ. Jesus Christ called us to work in His vineyard, which means we should be faithful in whatever office in the priesthood He has given us, because at the end of our work here on earth, we will be rewarded according to what each person did.

1 John 2:6 says: "Those who say they live in God should live their lives as Jesus did."

Hebrew 12:1-2 Apostle Paul wrote: "Therefore we also, since we are surrounded by so great a cloud of witnesses, let us lay aside every weight, and the sin which so easily ensnares us, and let us run with endurance the race that is set before us, looking unto Jesus, the author and finisher of our faith, who for the joy that was set before Him endured the cross, despising the shame, and has sat down at the right hand of the throne of God."

## Eli the priest

In 1 Samuel 2:12-35 and 1 Samuel 4:1-18, we read about Eli the priest, and the atrocities that his two sons, Hophni and Phinehas committed, and how God was very angry at them. Even though Eli didn't disobey God's commandments, God still held him responsible for what his children did because Eli was a priest, so He expected Eli to discipline His children which Eli failed to do. Even though Eli tried to talk to his sons, which they didn't listen; so Elohiym got angry and that was the end of their priesthood. The priesthood was supposed to continue in Eli's family but because of the evil Eli's sons committed, the priesthood was taken away from them and was given to Samuel. Eli's two sons were killed in the battlefield, and Eli also died after he heard about the news of the death of his two sons.

"Did I not choose him out of all the tribes of Israel to be My priest, to offer upon My altar, to burn incense, and to wear an ephod, before Me? And did I not give to the house of your father all the offerings of the children of Israel made by fire? Why do you kick at My offering which I have commanded in My dwelling place, and honour your sons more than Me, to make yourselves fat with the best of the offerings of Israel My people? Therefore, the LORD God of Israel says: 'I said indeed that your house and the house of your father would walk before Me forever.' But now the LORD says: 'Far be it from Me; for those who honour me I will honour, and those who despise Me shall be lightly esteemed. (1 Samuel 2:28-30).

1 Samuel 2:34-35 says: Now this shall be a sign to you that will come upon your two sons, on Hophni and Phinehas; in one day they shall die, both of them. Then I will raise up for Myself a faithful priest who shall do according to what is in My heart and mind. I will build him a sure house, and he shall walk before My anointed forever.

Revelation 22:12 says: "And behold, I am coming quickly, and My reward is with Me, to give to everyone according to his work. I am the Alpha and Omega, the Beginning and the End, the First and the Last."

Elohiym is still the same yesterday, today and forever! So as God's children, He wants us to live a certain lifestyle that would reflect Him to the world. We should continue to be steadfast in our faith, because at the end of this earthly journey, a crown is waiting for us. So many people started this race very well but along the way they sold their souls to the devil in exchange for wealth and fame; while some gave up because they didn't have the stamina to fight, and for others, their love for Adonai grew cold.

The reason people turn their back on our LORD Yahusha to worship Satan is because of greed, and they have no love and fear of God; it is only a very greedy person that would see hell and still decide to choose Satan because of the riches of this world that will not last; it is only a wicked person that will betray our LORD Yahusha, who died for the whole world to be saved, because of personal gain.

2 Timothy 4:6-8, Apostle Paul said: For I am already being poured out as a drink offering, and the time of my departure is at hand. I have fought the good fight, I have finished the race, I have kept the faith. Finally, there is laid up for me the crown of righteousness, which the LORD God Almighty, the righteous Judge,

will give to me on that day, and not to me only but also to all who have loved His appearing.

This statement of Apostle Paul should be the focus and priority of all believers. We are to finish what we were called to do as kings and priests; we should all strive for the crown that our LORD Adonai will give to us at the end of our journey here on earth. And not to follow the patterns of the world, we are set apart from the world, we are children of Elohiym, called to manifest His glory and power to this wicked world.

1 Corinthians 9-24-27 says: Do you not know that those who run in a race all run, but one receives the prize? Run in such a way that you may obtain it. And everyone who competes for the prize is temperate in all things. Now they do it to obtain a perishable crown, but we for an imperishable crown. Therefore, I run thus: not with uncertainty. Thus, I fight not as one who beats the air. But I discipline my body and bring it into subjection, lest, when I have preached to others, I myself should be disqualified.

1 Kings 13:1-34 tells a story about a Prophet that went from Judah to Bethel to declare the word of the LORD God Elohiym to Jeroboam and his evil altars. God commanded him not to eat or drink anything from Bethel nor return by the same way. But he disobeyed Elohiym; when an old Prophet heard about him, the old Prophet came to him and deceived him by telling him that God had spoken to him to tell this young man

of God that he can come home with him to eat and drink; and this young Prophet of Elohiym Yahuah believed the old retired Prophet and followed him to his house to eat and drink.

And while he was still eating, the old Prophet received a word from God, and he told this Prophet of God that he had contravened God's commandments and God's anger will rest upon him. So, on his way back home after eating and drinking, a lion met him and killed him according to the word of Elohiym. This Prophet, because of his disobedience to God's commandments, ended up not fulfilling his purpose and destiny, his priesthood office was cut off.

So many people started this race very well, but they are no longer on the side of our LORD God Yahusha Ha-Mashiach, they have fallen into the hands of the devil in exchange of wealth, while some have given up because they don't have the stamina to fight, because they don't have the revelation of our LORD God Ha-Mashiach! They are not rooted in the word of God; they weren't pruned and trained to stand steadfast in the faith when the enemies will come against them in different forms. So as sons and daughters of the Most High God Elohiym, we have to make sure we are rooted in His word and abide by them so that we can be able to discern between what God is saying and the lies the devil is speaking to us.

Mark 4:18-19 says: Now these are the ones sown among thorns; they are the ones who hear the word, and the cares of this world, the deceitfulness of riches, and the desires for other things entering in, choke the word, and it becomes unfruitful. (NKJV)

So be wise and follow the ways of the Holy Spirit, "He who has ears to hear, let him hear." (Mark 4:6)

# CHAPTER FOUR

# KNOWING YOUR TIME OF VISITATION

God's timing is quite different from our own timing! Elohiym created the whole world in His own timing; everything that we would become has already been written in His book. Therefore, it is left for us to discern it and use our time wisely to align with God's purpose. Every time we have is an opportunity for us to fulfil what we were assigned to fulfil. The saddest thing that would ever happen to anyone is to miss the time of their visitation. There are two things you can never get back once they've passed: The same opportunity, and time.

This is why it is very crucial we walk with the Holy Spirit, so that we can discern what God Adonai is doing in each time and season of our lives. Anytime we miss an opportunity, we might not get that same opportunity back, and in case we get another opportunity, we might have lost time. The reason many people are suffering today is because they have missed their time of visitation. That is why we have to be vigilant and be watchful because we don't know what day and hour our LORD God Yahusha Ha-Mashiach will visit us.

Christianity is not a religion; it is for all believers to have a relationship with God. So, for us not to miss our time of visitation, we must have a relationship with our Father God. When God created Adam and Eve and put them in the garden, they had a relationship with Him; He used to visit Adam and Eve in the garden of Eden until they sinned against Him and left God's presence (Genesis 3:8-13); and that was how they missed their visitation, the reason why they were created! The religious leaders, the Scribes and Pharisees and most people at the time of Jesus Christ's ministry on earth missed their time of visitation because they were just practising religion and not willing to humble themselves and obey His commandments! So, when Jesus Christ the Messiah came and told them that He is the Messiah, that they should believe in Him, they got offended and killed Him.

Luke 19:41-44: Now as He drew near, He saw the city and wept over it, saying, "If you had known, even you, especially in this your day, the things that make for you peace! But now they are hidden from your eyes. For days will come upon you when your enemies will build an embankment around you, surround you and close you in on every side, and level you, and your children within you, to the ground; and they will not leave in you one stone upon another, because you did not know the time of your visitation."

They rejected Yahusha the Messiah that came to save them, because of religion, they were not able to discern to see the signs that Jesus Christ is the Messiah the Prophets prophesied about. They were completely blind because of their wicked heart, so they refused to accept the truth. On several occasions Yahusha made it known to them that He is the Messiah. On one occasion, He told them that He is the Messiah they've been waiting for. "Your father Abraham rejoiced to see My day, and he saw it and was glad. Most assuredly, I say to you, before Abraham was, I AM." (John 8:56-58); But because of the hardness of their heart, they couldn't perceive Him, they didn't believe that Yahusha is God living among them. So, they missed the most significant thing in their lives, their time of visitation.

In Acts 7:51-52: Stephen addressing the Scribes and Pharisees: "You stiff-necked people, uncircumcised in heart and ears, you always resist the Holy Spirit. As your fathers did, so do you. Which of the Prophets did your fathers not persecute? And announced beforehand the coming of the Righteous One, whom you have now betrayed and murdered, you who received the law as delivered by angels and did not keep it."

As believers, we should know that life is spiritual; when we are conscious of spiritual things, things of the kingdom of God, our assignment on earth will be clear to us; we should refuse to dwell in the flesh because the flesh profits nothing! It will be difficult for us as believers to miss our time of visitation if we strive to walk faithfully with Adonai; this is how we can be able to discern in the spirit what God is doing in our lives, and also in the lives of our loved ones, and even our nation and intercede!

# Be wise and be prepared always

In Matthew 25:1-13; the parable of the ten virgins should compel us to be prepared at all times. "Then the Kingdom of heaven shall be likened to ten virgins who took their lamps and went out to meet the bridegroom. Now five of them were wise, and five were foolish. Those who were foolish took their lamps and took no oil with them, but the wise took oil in their vessels with their lamps. But while the bridegroom was delayed, they all slumbered and slept. "And at midnight a cry was heard; 'Behold, the bridegroom is coming; go out to meet him!' Then all those virgins arose and trimmed their lamps. And the foolish said to the wise, 'Give us some of your oil, for our lamps are going out.' But the wise answered, saying, 'No, lest there should not be enough for us and you; but go rather to those who sell, and buy for yourselves.' And while they went to buy, the bridegroom came, and those who were ready went in with him to the wedding; and the door was shut. "Afterward the other virgins came also, saying, 'LORD, LORD, open to us!' But he answered and said, 'Assuredly, I say to you, I do not know you.' "Watch therefore, for you know neither the day nor the hour in which the Son of Man is coming.

    We understand by Scripture that the bridegroom is Yahusha Ha-Mashiach, and the virgins were His brides, the believers. Five virgins were said to be wise: they were prepared, they had extra oil in their vessels, they were the watchmen, the intercessors that were walking faithfully with God, keeping His commandments. While the other five virgins were foolish; they were believers that had no extra oil in their vessels: they were not prepared, they didn't have a relationship with the Holy Spirit, they were empty! So, when the hour of their visitation came, the five wise virgins that were prepared, keeping God's commandments faithfully, went in with the LORD God Yahusha, the bridegroom, to the feast.

    These five virgins had a relationship with the Holy Spirit and walked with Him faithfully! These are the believers striving in the spirit, redeeming the time! So, their vessel was full of oil and that was why they didn't miss their time of visitation. On the other hand, the five foolish virgins were believers who refused to grow in the things of the spirit, they never had a relationship with Yahusha, their vessels were empty, they were not watchful in prayers, and they were not abiding by the commandments of God! They were enjoying the pleasures of the world; they couldn't discern the time and be prepared to meet with the Messiah. So, they missed the most significant moment of their lives, their time of visitation!

Most believers today are still living as unbelievers! The things of God Elohiym are not their priority, the commandments of God are not important to them; so, they refuse to grow in their relationship with God. They are like the five foolish virgins; they just bear the title; I am a Christian. They don't want to come out of their comfort zone and seek His presence, His guidance, to transform to become who He has called them to be. If the Israelites, the Jewish leaders had repented from their wicked ways and accepted Yahusha as their Messiah, they wouldn't have missed their time of visitation when He came to them on this earth.

For you not to miss your hour of visitation, and to fulfil your purpose here on earth, there are things you must do to achieve that.

1. You must repent and come back to Jesus Christ if you haven't done so and walk with Him faithfully. You must always listen to the instructions of the Holy Spirit and put Him first in everything that you do.

2. You must spend quality time with the word of Elohiym, until the word of God becomes part of you. The Bible told us in John 1:1 that Yahusha is the word of God, so the more of God's word you have in your spirit, the more Yahusha will become real to you. A believer that doesn't have the word of Elohiym in their spirit will be like the five foolish virgins that had no oil in their vessels.

3. You must constantly watch and pray with all manners of prayers and fasting. Ephesians 6:18 says: Praying always with all prayers and supplications in the Spirit, being watchful to this end with all perseverance and supplication for all the saints.

Matthew 26:41 says: To watch and pray that you may not enter into temptation. The spirit indeed is willing, but the flesh is weak.

4. You must always do the work of evangelism. 2 Timothy 4:5 says: As for you, always be sober-minded, endure suffering, do the work of an evangelist, and fulfil your ministry.

Proverbs 11:30 says: The fruit of the righteous is a tree of life, and whoever wins souls is wise.

We must live a life of total obedience, be filled with the fruit of the Spirit, and persevere always to fulfil our assignment which the LORD God has given us. Any believer that does these things will never miss their appointed time with the LORD God Almighty Elohiym. There's no way you will be faithful to God's commandments and Adonai will not be faithful to His promises towards you. There's no believer who spends quality time in praying and fasting seeking His presence, being in a relationship with Adonai that would not fulfil what has been assigned for him or her to fulfil.

Proverbs 3:5-6 says: Trust in El-Yahuah with all thine heart; and lean not unto your own understanding. In all thy ways acknowledge Him, and he shall direct thy paths (CEPHER).

The reason the five wise virgins were able to wait till the end was because they put all their trust in Jesus Christ. They persevered continually in the spirit to keep their vessels filled with oil! Even when sometimes they might feel tired and weak, still they kept on praying and waiting patiently upon the Messiah, obeying His commandments. If the wise men did not know and understand the times and seasons, they would have missed the most precious time in their lives of meeting with the Messiah at His birth! The reason Daniel knew the time Israel will be visited, and the holy city will be rebuilt was because He was constantly studying the word of God, praying, watching and striving in the spirit (Daniel 9:1-27).

The woman with the issue of blood was able to discern the time of her visitation because she was prepared. She had wasted twelve years going to the wrong places for her healing, and all was in vain! But when she heard testimonies of how Yahusha had been healing people, she said to herself that this was her moment too, her visitation had come! She had been waiting for this moment, and she was not ready to miss it! She kept on praying and waiting upon Yahusha Adonai! Finally, when Yahusha was passing by the town she was living in, she immediately rose up and went to meet with the Messiah!

The Scriptures say it wasn't easy, but she had determined in her heart that that was the day of her visitation; regardless of the odour that was coming out from her body, she refused to be distracted; She pressed into the crowd just to touch the hem of Yahusha's garment! And as soon as she touched the hem of His garment, she was made whole completely! (Mark 5:25-34).

If this woman wasn't prepared, she would have missed the time of her visitation! The Bible said she had suffered from many physicians and her case rather grew worse. In that situation you're in, what are you doing for the LORD God Yahusha to visit you? Are you spending quality time in His word? Are you waiting upon Him? Is your mindset renewed? Is it based upon the word of God? Or your mind is focused upon the things that are happening around your life? If this is the case, then you have to repent and focus on Adonai, your Creator. Hold on to the faith, no matter the challenges that you are facing in life, because your time of visitation is just around the corner.

Romans 13:11 says: And do this, understanding the present time; the hour has already come for you to wake up from your slumber, because our salvation is nearer now than when we first believed.

## The Time is closer than you think

We are living in the end time of the age! Jesus Christ spoke about it in Matthew 24:1-51. Based on this

Scripture we should be prepared and be watchful because we do not know the hour at which the LORD God will return. When you don't have a relationship with the Holy Spirit, and walk faithfully by His word, how can you know and follow the direction He is guiding you to?

Matthew 24:37-39 says: As the days of Noah were, so will the coming of the Son of Man be. For as in those days which were before the flood they were eating and drinking, marrying and giving in marriage, until the day that Noah entered into the ship, and they didn't know until the flood came and took them all away, so will the coming of the Son of Man be.

Is it not what is happening now with most people all over the world? Drinking and getting drunk, living a life of immorality! Selling their precious souls to the devil, because they are still living in the flesh. They prefer to dwell in the flesh than to grow in the spirit. These are the kind of people that would miss their time of visitation if they don't repent and live for Yahusha; in verse 42, Elohiym instructed us to watch therefore, for we do not know in what hour He will come.

Matthew 24:43-50: Jesus Christ continues to speak in parables. "But know this, that if the master of the house had known on what watch of the night the thief was coming, he would have watched and would not have allowed his house to be broken into. Therefore, also be ready, for in an hour that you don't expect, the Son of Man will come. "Who then is the faithful and wise servant, whom his lord has set over his household, to give them their food in due season? Blessed is that servant whom his lord finds doing so when he comes. Most certainly I tell you that he will set him over all that he has. But if that evil servant should say in his heart, 'My lord is delaying his coming,' and begins to beat his fellow servants, and eat and drink with the drunkards, the lord of that servant will come in a day when he doesn't expect it and in an hour when he doesn't know it, and will cut him in pieces and appoint his portion with the hypocrites. That is where the weeping and grinding of teeth will be.

Because of the pleasures of this world, many believers including leaders and ministers of the gospel have missed their time of visitation, they have missed their purpose in life. They have sold their souls to the devil in exchange for wealth and power. And the worst part is that they are initiating as many believers as they can to the devil in order for them to continue to enjoy their wealth and use their evil powers to deceive and destroy gullible Christians. The youths of this generation are far from knowing the true God that created them. People are living as if there is no God, they have become their own god, living a life of lawlessness.

Matthew 24:11-12 says: Then many false Prophets will rise up and deceive many. And because lawlessness will abound, the love of many will grow cold.

## Impatience destroys great destinies

Elohiym made a covenant with Abraham, He promised Abraham in Genesis 17:16-19, that he was going to have a son, and his name would be called Isaac. Abraham and Sarah waited for so many years patiently for the promise to come to pass. And when Sarah had given up on having a child because of her old age, Sarah convinced her husband Abraham to have a child with Hagar, her maidservant, which Abraham did and Hagar conceived and gave Abraham a son called Ishmael (Genesis 16:1-12). But God told Abraham that Ishmael is not the promised son, and that Abraham will have a child with Sarah. Because of impatience, Sarah convinced her husband Abraham to have a child with her maidservant, which brought a lot of disunity. So many believers have made a lot of wrong choices because of impatience which has caused them to lose their time of visitation; God's plans for their lives, and even loss of loved ones.

Genesis 18:1-15 says three angels visited Abraham and Sarah, which many biblical scholars believed that one of them was the LORD God, and the LORD told Abraham the good news that Sarah would conceive and give birth to a child and his name shall be called Isaac. God finally answered Abraham's prayer after Abraham had walked faithfully with God believing Him that He will never fail him concerning His promise on his life. The reason Abraham could recognise that it was the LORD God Almighty was because he had a relationship with Him, that was why as soon as Adonai appeared to him, he immediately responded to Him. He would have missed the day of his visitation if he hadn't had a relationship with God and to discern that this is the LORD God Almighty that came to visit him with His two angels (cf. Gen 18:1-17).

Faith has the power to shape our destinies if we walk by it. Through Abraham's lineage, the Messiah, our Saviour was born, opening the door for all humans to be saved through one man, Yahusha Ha-Mashiach. There is no way your entire life will remain the same again when the Messiah visits you. You will become a different person after your encounter with Him. So let all your focus be on the Messiah because your time of visitation is at hand.

Job 10:12 says: You have granted me life and loving kindness. Your visitation has preserved my spirit. (WMB)

## Zacchaeus' encounter with Jesus

Luke 19:2-10: Zacchaeus is another man that Yahusha Elohiym visited because of his amazing faith. Zacchaeus was a covetous man, a tax collector that uses his authority to extort people's money. Because of his wicked actions, people in that city hated him. But one faithful day Zacchaeus heard that Yahusha was passing by his town and Zacchaeus decided to climb a tree in order to see Jesus because of the crowd and because of his height. And when Yahusha saw his faith, what he had to do to see Him, Yahusha called him to come down.

And when Yahusha came to the place Zacchaeus was, He looked up and saw Zacchaeus on the tree, Yahusha was touched by the faith of Zacchaeus and said to him, "Zacchaeus, make haste and come down, for today I must stay at your house," Zacchaeus' faith paves the way for the Messiah to visit him and his household that day. A sinner that everyone despised became a new man. Yahusha became his guest, everyone that was there that claimed to be righteous didn't have this honour of Adonai being their guest.

Zacchaeus believed in Yahusha and was humbled, he put away his pride and repented of all his sins and promised to return back fourfold of all the money that he had taken from people and to give half of his goods to the poor. Our humility attracts God's visitation. When we humble ourselves before the Lord God Yahusha and obey His commandments, He visits us.

## God despises the man with pride

Pride is one of the greatest sins that has stopped so many people from having an encounter with the LORD God Almighty. If Elisha was proud, he would have missed his time of visitation when Elijah told him and his other servants not to follow him, but Elisha among all the other servants insisted that he would follow his master Elijah to the end; and that was how Elijah transferred his anointing to Elisha while the other servants of Elijah remained in the position they were (2 King 2:1-15). The decisions you make in life determine your ability to discern your future! And you can only perceive when you have the ability to discern. Many believers have missed their time of visitation because of lack of discernment!

The Scripture says in James 4:6: But He gives more grace. Therefore, He says: "God resists the proud, but gives grace to the humble."

James 4:10: says: Humble yourselves in the sight of the Lord God, and He will lift you up.

Philippians 1:9-10 says: "And it is my prayer that your love may abound more and more, with knowledge and all discernment, so that you may approve what is excellent, and so be pure and blameless for the day of Christ.

The reason why the church of Yahusha Adonai is not manifesting the glory of God as Elohiym has promised the church in His word is because most people are still operating in pride. Amos 3:3 says: can two walk together, except they be agreed! We can only walk with God when we act like Him; when we allow Him to guide us! God opposes the proud and embraces the humble. People that are humble always find favour in the sight of God! There are times God Adonai will give someone instruction to do something, but because of pride and greed, the person will miss what God intended to do in that person's life.

Your attitude will determine how far you will go in the kingdom of God! If Mary, the mother of Yahusha on earth, wasn't humble, she would've missed her time of visitation! Your determination can change things in the realm of the spirit to your favour! And gratitude prompts God to visit your situation.

Let's look at what the Messiah said about the Pharisee and the tax collector that went to pray in Luke 18:9-14: The Pharisee and the tax collector went to the temple to pray. The Pharisee was self-righteous and full of pride, claiming to be better than the tax collector; he thanked God Elohiym that he wasn't a sinner like the tax collector. While the tax collector on the other hand humbled himself knowing that he was a sinner that needed God's mercies, bowed down his head, refused to look into heaven and prayed for God to have mercy upon him. Yahusha Adonai says that it was the tax collector who went home justified because of his humility.

Luke 18:14: I tell you; this man went down to his house justified rather than the other; for everyone who exalts himself will be humbled, and he who humbles himself will be exalted."

The only way for us as believers not to miss our time of visitation is when we completely lay aside every pride and self-righteousness and totally surrender to the will of our LORD God Adonai the Messiah. We have read in the Bible that, all Scripture is God-breathed and is useful for teaching, rebuking, correcting and training in righteousness, so that the servant of God may be thoroughly equipped for every good work (2 Timothy 3:16-17)

May the LORD God Almighty Elohiym remember and visit you as you surrender and keep His commandments. Amen.

# CHAPTER FIVE

# DIVINE PRESENCE OF GOD

The presence of Elohiym finds its greatest expression in Immanuel, God with us. God's presence is what makes the difference in every situation that we would face in life. Without the presence of the Almighty God, no believer can be able to superimpose any authority over the powers of the kingdom of darkness. It is the presence of God that a believer carries that will enable the believer to live a life of constant victory. The purpose of God creating man is for man to carry His presence, manifest His power and bring glory to Him.

Genesis 1:26-27: God said, "Let Us make man in Our image, according to Our likeness; let them have dominion over the fish of the sea, over the birds of the air, and over the cattle, over all the earth and over every creeping thing that creeps on the earth." So, God created man in His own image; in the image of God, He created him; male and female He created them. Then God blessed them, and God said to them, "Be fruitful and multiply; fill the earth and subdue it; have dominion over the fish of the sea, over the birds of the air, and over every living thing that moves on the earth."

The plan of Elohiym for humanity is for us to exercise dominion over everything that He has created in order to bring glory to His Holy name. After God had created man, He then put them in the garden of Eden. The garden of Eden represents a place of preface peace and fulfilment, time to time, Yahuah would come to Eden to visit Adam and spend time with him and his wife until Adam and Eve sinned against God by going against His commandment and they were driven out of the garden of Eden and were separated from God's presence. The Scriptures said from that day on, sin came into the world.

## God's intervention

When sin came into the world, man was separated from Elohiym. So, God had to intervene in order to bring man back to His divine presence and purpose by coming to this earth to die for all humans, so as to bring us back to Himself.

John 3:16: "For God so loved the world, that He gave His only Son, that whoever believes in Him should not perish but have eternal life."

Yahusha Ha-Mashiach came and restored us back to our Father God Yahuah! Now we can boldly go into His presence and not be afraid. Nothing in this world can be compared to God's divine presence. People that despise God's presence and seek to be in the presence of Satan have completely lost their mind. What is in this world that would make anyone reject God's presence and prefer to work for the devil? When I see some people that are living without the presence of Elohiym, it saddens me! I have come across many preachers that carry the presence of Satan instead of the presence of the Most High God.

Thank God for the gift of discernment, if not I would've died long ago. But because of God's faithfulness and love; He delivered me from the hands of all those false ministers. The body of Christ that is supposed to stand and operate in God's power and bring His kingdom down is sleeping in the realm of the spirit. The whole world is filled with all forms of wickedness and immorality! No one can carry the presence of the Almighty God Elohiym without total obedience to God's word! It is through His divine presence we can fulfil our divine purpose here on earth.

In Genesis 3:6, we read that when Eve saw that the tree was good for food, that it was pleasant to the eyes, and a tree desirable to make one wise, she took of its fruit and ate. She also gave it to her husband with her, and he ate it.

We are in this world but not of this world! Our desires should be in the things of God Almighty and not in the things of this world that would perish soon; the moment we put our desires on the things of this world, we will definitely sell our soul to the devil. God's plan is for us to be blessed in every area of our lives, but He can only bless us with what we need, by abiding in His divine presence. He empowered and blessed Adam and Eve with everything they needed, but because of the desires of the eyes and greed, they wanted to be like Elohiym their Creator, they fell into the trap the devil set for them and for all human, and they lost the most valuable thing in their life, the divine presence of the most high God.

1 John 2:16-17 says: For all that is in the world-the desires of the flesh and the desires of the eyes and pride of life-is not from the Father but is from the world. And the world is passing away along with its desires, but whoever does the will of God abides forever.

Proverbs 27:20 says: "Hell and destruction are never full; so, the eyes of man are never satisfied."

In Genesis 3:7-8, we read that as soon as Adam and Eve disobeyed Elohiym by obeying the voice of the devil, their eyes were both opened, and they knew that they were naked, and they made fig leaves to cover up their body. And when they heard the sound of Elohiym walking in the garden in the cool of the day, Adam and his wife hid themselves from the presence of Elohiym because they couldn't be in His presence anymore because sin had separated them from coming into His presence.

Adam and Eve shifted their focus from God Almighty who had created them, put them in the garden of Eden and had given Adam authority and power to rule as king and priest. This is exactly what is happening in our world today! God has given us His power and authority to rule as kings and priests, but some people prefer to dwell in darkness and be a slave to the devil because of the riches of this world than to dwell in the presence of Elohiym and rule as king and priest!

John 3:19 says: And this is the condemnation, that the Light has come into the world, and men loved darkness rather than light, because their deeds were evil.

Adam and Eve had a wonderful relationship with God in the garden of Eden until they diverted their desires from being in the divine presence of God to the desires of the flesh, which cost them total separation from the divine presence of God. When I look at the body of Christ today which He bought with His precious blood, it grieves me! When I see some ministers preaching another gospel, instead of the gospel of the cross, it makes me really sad. For us to see revival in this end time, the body of Christ has to repent from all kinds of immoralities and wickedness and surrender totally to Christ. Each time I go to any of the social media platforms, When I hear what some ministers of the gospel are preaching and doing, it's really disgusting, bringing shame to the Holy name of our LORD God Yahusha Ha-Mashiach.

Apostle Paul emphasises it clearly to us in Romans 6:23: For the wages of sin is death, but the gift of God is eternal life in Christ Jesus our LORD.

## The presence of Elohiym is our shield

The presence of God is the means and end of redemption! The Almighty God steps in to pay the price, to redeem man's sin and ensure his purposes. The Creator becomes a covenant Redeemer; Christ the Son of God Elohiym, entered human history to give His life as a ransom for many that would believe in Him. Through His abundance of grace and mercies, Christ reconciles us to Himself, and re-opens access to the Father Yahuah Elohiym so that those who were once exiled from His presence might again draw near to God. His presence is our shield!

Hebrews 7:19 says: For the priestly regimen made nothing perfect, but the bringing in of a better hope; By which we draw nigh unto Elohiym (CEPHER)

Throughout Scriptures we have read that the power of God is in His presence. We are nothing without His presence, it doesn't matter how wealthy, or how intelligent, or how good looking you are, without God's presence in your life, you cannot manifest His glory and be fulfilled in life.

The Psalmist wrote it this way in Psalms 127:1-2: Unless the LORD God builds the house, they labour in vain who build it; Unless the LORD God guards the city, the watchmen stay awake in vain. It is vain for you to rise up early, to sit up late, to eat the bread of sorrows; For so He gives His beloved sleep.

As believers we cannot do anything successfully without His divine presence in our lives. This is why we cannot joke with His commandments! Towards the end of Yahusha's ministry on earth, He promised His disciples that He will send them a Comforter that will be with them and will guide them to all truth. Jesus knew that without His presence with us, we will be like a sheep without a shepherd; we won't make it in this wicked world we are living in.

In John 14:15-18, Jesus speaks: "If you love Me, keep My commandments. And I will pray to the Father, and He will give you another Helper, that He may abide with you forever-the Spirit of truth, whom the world cannot receive, because it neither sees Him nor knows Him, but you knows Him, for He dwells with you and will be in you. I will not leave you orphans; I will come to you.

Our LORD Yahusha made it clear in His words that the only way we can abide in His presence, is when we keep His commandments! Look at what the Prophets and the Apostles in the Bible did, they did incredible things because they carried the presence of God by obeying His laws. For a believer to be filled with the Spirit of God, that person needs the presence of

Elohiym. For a believer to operate in the gifts of the Spirit written in 1 Corinthians 12:7-11, that person needs the presence of God Adonai.

We have a lot of baby Christians today in the body of Christ, and until the body of Christ grows up to become sons and daughters, the church will not manifest the power and the glory of God. Apostle Paul carried the presence of God so much that even handkerchiefs that were brought from his body healed the sick and demons were leaving people. He didn't need to lay hands on anyone. This is the Dunamis of God being demonstrated by Paul.

Acts 19:11-12: Now God worked unusual miracles by the hands of Paul, so that even handkerchiefs or aprons were brought from his body to the sick, and the diseases left them, and the evil spirits went out of them.

Believers are all over the world, but they are not serious in keeping the commandments of God. This is why the church is finding it hard to make a great impact in this world, most especially in this end time; every believer has a role to play in order to bring change to this dying world. In the days of the early church, the Apostles of Yahusha did the impossible for the kingdom of God because they were all carrying the glorious presence of Elohiym; they were submissive to the Holy Spirit! There was nothing they could do without inquiring from the Holy Spirit. They only did what the Holy Spirit asked them to do; that was why

God Yahusha Elohiym did unusual miracles through them. But many followers of Christ today do things without inquiring from the Holy Spirit. So, the Holy Spirit is not there in their midst to glorify the name of Yahusha.

The Apostles were so filled with the Spirit of Yahusha Elohiym that many signs and wonders were done by them! They brought Heaven down on earth; the Scribes and Pharisees were afraid of them because these men were all on fire. There was no kind of miracles these men didn't do; God Elohiym honoured His words in their mouth; why? Because they honoured Yahusha Ha-Mashiach with their life! People all over were bringing all manners of sick people for them to heal them and none of those sick people went back home the same way they came. The shadow of Peter was healing the sick that were laid on the streets and demons were leaving their bodies. Every day, believers were added to them because of the presence of God they carried. It is the presence of Adonai that a believer carries that would draw multitude to Jesus Christ. It is not by our own power to draw multitudes to Christ! It is the presence of God that we carry that would draw the multitude to Yahusha (Acts 5:12-17)

This is the kind of power God wants His church to operate at. If the church was operating at this high level of God's power, do you think this world would be the way it is today? The body of Christ seriously needs the presence of Elohiym!

In John 14:12 Jesus speaks: "Most assuredly, I say to you, he who believes in Me, the works that I do he will do also; and greater works than these he will do, because I go to My Father.

So many ministers of the gospel have turned themselves to become the almighty. They have diverted the hearts of their congregations towards themselves. Their congregations worship them instead of our Father and Saviour, Yahusha Ha-Mashiach, and this is why we have a lot of babies in the body of Christ today. And the reason so many believers are being oppressed by the enemies is because they are not equipped with the word of God in order to carry His presence. Until you're equipped with the true word of God, you will not prevail over the kingdom of darkness. And for this reason, the Holy Spirit is grieved because He came to empower us so that we can fulfil our mission on earth and bring glory and honour to the Holy name of Yahusha Ha-Mashiach.

When you look at what is happening all over the world, you may be wondering, where is God? But the problem is not Elohiym because God has warned us of what is going to happen if we fail to walk in His commandments. So instead of blaming God for the terrible things happening all over the world, we should go on our knees and repent of our sins and mistakes, so that He can heal the land.

The Prophets and the Apostles in the Bible cherished the presence of God Elohiym so much that they could pay any price just to dwell in the presence of

God. Today, many believers hardly care about the presence of God, they rather care about the things of the world and how to please themselves rather than to please God!

1 Corinthians 2:9 says: "But as it is written, eye hath not seen, nor ear heard; Neither have entered into the heart of man, the things which God hath prepared for them that love Him."

Psalm 16:11 says: Thou wilt show me the path of life; in thy presence is fullness of joy; in thy right hand there are pleasures forevermore.

Do you think without the divine presence of Elohiym the Most High God that was with Moses, he would have been able to deliver the children of Israel from the hand of Pharaoh? When God told Moses that He would send him to Pharaoh to bring His people out of Egypt, Moses was afraid because of Pharaoh! He knew he would not survive in the presence of Pharaoh, because he was a wanted man, and also because he had a speech disorder, so he would find it difficult to communicate clearly to Pharaoh, (Exodus 4:10). So, he said, "LORD, who am I? That I should go unto Pharaoh, and deliver your people?" (cf. Exodus 3:10-11).

And God said, "surely I will be with thee; and this shall be a token unto thee: When thou hast brought forth the people out of Egypt, ye shall serve Elohiym upon this mountain." (Exodus 3:12) Before the children of Israel left Egypt, they saw the power of the presence of God mightily! They saw how God fought their battle for them. At midnight the children of God witnessed how God smote all the firstborn in the land of Egypt, from the firstborn of Pharaoh that sat on his throne unto the firstborn of the captive that was in the dungeon; and all the firstborn of cattle, and how God protected them from all the plagues that He brought to the land of Egypt, God brought complete judgement to the people of Egypt (Exodus 12:21-29).

Pharaoh wouldn't have let the children of Israel go if he hadn't seen the power of the presence of the Almighty God. All of Pharaoh's magicians failed to deliver the land from the mighty power of God; they did everything they could but failed. After God had done the last plague by killing all the firstborn of Egypt, that was when Pharaoh decided to let the children of God go! The presence of Elohiym brought them out from the hands of their enemies. And it was the presence of God that parted the red sea for them to walk on dry land and drowned all Pharaoh's men in the red sea (Exodus 14:13-31).

The word of God in Romans 8:31 says: "What shall we then say to these things? If God be for us, who can be against us?" No matter what you are going through, if you seek the presence of God with all your heart, you will surely come out of that situation. Do you know what it takes to part the sea? If the presence of Elohiym was not with Moses, do you think the Red Sea would have parted? We are not talking of a small cup of water poured on a ground, even with that, no man can be able to part it without the Supernatural power of God.

According to Exodus 12:37, we know that about six hundred thousand men besides women and children, flocks and herds walked on dry land through the midst of the Red Sea. And as soon as they had crossed to the other side of the Sea, the LORD God Almighty told Moses to stretch out his rod towards the Red Sea, and the Sea returned to its original state and covered all the Egyptian army, chariots and horsemen and they all died. This is what the divine presence of God did for the children of Israel (Exodus 14:1-31).

The divine presence of Elohiym can break any mountain into pieces, His presence makes a way where there seems to be no way. Psalm 97:5 says: The mountains melt like wax before the LORD, before the LORD of all the earth.

Matthew 21:44 says; "And whosoever shall fall on this Stone shall be broken but on whomsoever it shall fall, it will grind him to powder."

The stone in this Scripture is Yahusha Ha-Mashiach! When you read the story of David and how he killed Goliath, you will realise that all we need on this earth to overcome every battle is the divine presence of God. David understood the Scriptures and that was why he used the five stones in killing Goliath (1 Samuel 17:40-51). David understood that if not for the presence of God that was with him, he wouldn't have been able to kill the lion and the bear when they came and took a lamb out of the flock when he was looking after them.

So, when David heard what the Philistine said about God, in verses 10 and 23 saying "I defy the armies of Israel this day; give me a man, that we may fight together." He became so angry, and he said, "For who is this uncircumcised Philistine, that he should defy the armies of the living God?" (Verse 26). Therefore, when Saul heard about the boldness of David, he sent for him and David, full of God's presence, said to Saul; "don't be afraid, I will fight this Philistine." (Verse 32). David was so bold that even Saul couldn't believe it.

1 Samuel 17:34-37: But David said to Saul, "Your servant used to keep his father's sheep, and when a lion or a bear came and took a lamb out of the flock, I went out after it and struck it, and delivered the lamb from its mouth; and when it arose against me, I caught it by its beard, and struck and killed it. Your servant has killed both lion and bear; and this uncircumcised Philistine will be like one of them, seeing he has defied the armies of the living God." Moreover, David said, "The LORD, who delivered me from the paw of the lion and from the paw of the bear, He will deliver me from the hand of this Philistine." And Saul said to David, "Go, and the LORD God be with you!"

All the people of Israel were so afraid that no one was able to face the Philistine except David because he knew the God of Abraham, Isaac and Jacob. He had a relationship with Elohiym. He had seen the mighty power of God in his life and how He had delivered the lion and the bear into his hand. Are you confident in the God of Abraham, Isaac and Jacob that created the entire world? Because your confidence in Elohiym determines your reaction when you face storms.

In verse 38, we read how Saul put all his armour for the battle on David, he wore his helmet of brass on David's head; he also put on his coat of mail on David; but David declined using them, he had already told Saul that the God who saved him from the lion, bear and other wild animals while watching over his father's sheep will surely deliver the Philistine into his hand. Why? Because he knew the presence of the LORD God was with him. He knew he had a relationship with the LORD God Almighty. In verses 40-50, David took five smooth stones from the brook, along with his sling, and used the stone in killing Goliath.

Verses 45-47; Then David said to the Philistine, "You come to me with a sword, with a spear, and with javelin. But I come to you in the name of the LORD of Hosts, the God of the armies of Israel, whom you have defiled. This day the LORD God will deliver you into my hand, and I will strike you and take your head from you. And this day I will give the carcasses of the camp of the Philistines to the birds of the air and the wild beasts of the earth, that all the earth may know that there is a God in Israel. Then all this assembly shall know that the LORD God does not save with sword and spear; for the battle is the LORD's, and He will give you into our hands." It is only when you know the living God Elohiym and you are walking in obedience to His words, that you will be able to have this kind of boldness.

A young man called David who hasn't been to any war nor fought any battle before had the boldness to say he will kill the Philistine giant and give his body to the birds of the air. On the other hand, all the Philistines knew Goliath that he had never been defeated in any battle before! Even Saul and all the people of Israel were afraid of this giant named Goliath, because they heard him boasting about how no man in Israel would be able to fight him, and they knew that Goliath had been fighting battles for a long time and has always prevailed.

I Samuel 17:8-11: Then he stood and cried out to the armies of Israel, and said to them, "Why have you come out to line up for battle? Am I not a Philistine, and you the servants of Saul? Choose a man for yourselves and let him come down to me. If he is able to fight with me and kill me, then we will be your servants. But if I prevail against him and kill him, then you shall be our servants and serve us." And the Philistine said, "I defy the armies of Israel this day; give me a man, that we may fight together." When Saul and all Israel heard these words of the Philistine, they were dismayed and greatly afraid.

David was the only man in the whole land of Israel to challenge Goliath and said he would kill him and give him to the birds of the air to feed on; and that was exactly what happened. Did you see the courage, the faith and trust, and the boldness David had in Elohiym;

Tell me? Why won't God honour His name? The reason God Almighty Elohiym has not moved in that situation you're going through is because, you put your trust in man, in your wisdom, in the economy of this earth; and because you are afraid of the Goliath that has been defying the name of the Most high God in your life, you have kept quiet; instead of getting angry like David and say to the devil, "The LORD Elohiym rebuke you."

Daniel 11:32: Those who do wickedly against the covenant he shall corrupt with flattery; but the people who know their God shall be strong and carry out great exploits.

There's no way you will be afraid of any giants when you know the Almighty God Elohiym and have a perfect relationship with Him. The reason many Christians are so afraid of the devil is because they don't know the God of Abraham, Isaac, and Jacob! And there is no way you will carry the presence of God when you don't know Him. Even though He is in you, as a child of Elohiym, He will be quiet, until you begin to engage in doing what He has commanded you to do.

In verse 49, when the Philistine arose and came and drew near to meet David, that David hurried and ran toward the Philistine; then David put his hand in his bag and took out a stone; and he slung it and struck the Philistine in his forehead, so that the stone sank into his forehead, and he fell on his face to the earth. If you ever want to prevail over those enemies that are coming against you, then you must learn how to trust God completely and obey His commandments, that is the only way God will move, because of your trust and faith in Him. If David had accepted all the armours of Saul that was given to him to fight Goliath, God wouldn't have fought for him; God saw the trust and confidence David had in Him, so God acted according to that. On the other hand, Goliath was well armed with all manners of weapon to fight the battle, and it didn't scare David a bit.

"For the LORD God will not forsake His people, for His great name's sake, because it has pleased the LORD God to make you, His people." 1 Samuel 12:22.

"Elohim Yahuah can never forsake all those who seek Him diligently."

In Verses 50-51: So, David prevailed over the Philistine with a sling and a stone and struck the Philistine and killed him. But there was no sword in the hand of David. Therefore, David ran and stood over the Philistine, took his sword and drew it out of its sheath and killed him, and cut off his head with it. And when the Philistines saw that their champion was dead, they fled.

Just as Elohiym used the rod in Moses' hands to do great signs and wonders in the land of Egypt and also used the rod to part the Red Sea, likewise, He used the stone that was in the hand of David to bring down the giant of the Philistine. So, it is your faith in God that would move God to cut off the head of the strongman that has been attacking you.

Matthew 21:44: "And whoever falls on this stone will be broken; but on whomever it falls, it will grind him to powder."

There was great peace in the land of Israel after David had killed Goliath and all the Philistines fled. God Almighty Elohiym brought victory to the people of Israel and His name was glorified. People that really know and trust God are never afraid whenever the enemies come against them because they already know what Elohiym will do to them. For God to allow battles to come your way means He has chosen to use you as His battle axe.

Jeremiah 51:20-24: God speaks: "You are My battle axe and weapons of war; For with you I will break the nation in pieces; With you I will destroy kingdoms: With you I will break in pieces the horse and its rider; With you also I will break in pieces man and woman; With you I will break in pieces old and young; With you I will break in pieces the young man and the maiden; With you also I will break in pieces the shepherd and his flock; With you I will break in pieces the farmer and his yoke of oxen; And with you I will break in pieces governors and rulers. "And I will repay Babylon and all the inhabitants of Chaldea for all the evil they have done in Zion in your sight," says the LORD God of Host.

1 Corinthians 2:9 says: "But as it is written, Eye has not seen, nor ear heard, neither have entered into the heart of man, the things which Elohiym has prepared for them that love Him." (CEPHER)

Absolutely nothing in this world can be compared to the divine presence of Elohiym. Whoever carries the presence of God is a terror to the kingdom of darkness, because our God is a consuming fire. That is the reason the devil does not want anybody to know the truth. Because the truth you know determines the level of God's presence you carry, and that was why Moses, the Apostles and the Prophets in the Bible carried so much of God's power. Always remember, that the bigger the test, the greater the anointing! So, stop running away from the battle! Confront it, and you shall see the victory of the LORD God Almighty Elohiym.

## The benefits of the presence of Elohiym in our lives.

- The presence of God gives you divine direction (Exodus 13:20-21; Proverbs 3:5-6; Psalm 23).
- The presence of God gives you revelation of who Christ is (Matthew 16:13-17).
- The presence of God gives you supernatural boldness (2 Timothy 1:7; Acts 4:29-31; Ephesians 3:12).
- The presence of God activates supernatural supplies. It is impossible to be lacking when you

carry God's presence. (John 2:1-11; Luke 5:1-7; Matthew 14:13-21; Mark 8:1-9).

- The presence of God in your life creates signs and wonders and brings healing to your body and to others around you. (Acts 14:8-10; Hebrews 2:4).

- The presence of God imparts supernatural strength for victory in battle. 1 Samuel 30:1-19; Judges 7:1-25).

- The presence of God opens impossible doors for you. The story of Joseph is one great story that illustrates that God can do anything for those that keep His commandments. In Genesis chapters 37 to 41, we read how Joseph's brothers sold him into slavery at the age of 17 out of jealousy-jealousy of their father's love for him and of his dreams. Joseph was accused by Potiphar's wife and was sent to prison. Joseph in the prison began interpreting dreams for the prisoners, which established his reputation as a great interpreter.

Pharaoh called on Joseph to interpret his dreams and was impressed with Joseph's wisdom and counsel. Pharaoh then appointed Joseph as second-in-command and gave him the name Zaphenath-Paneah. Pharaoh then put Joseph in charge of his court and the entire land of Egypt; he even put his signet ring on Joseph's finger. As Prime Minister, Joseph carried out all the economic reforms to prevent the disaster

Pharaoh's dream foretold and demonstrated God's concern for all peoples.

- The presence of God brings you peace and joy. Romans 15:13 says: May the God of hope fill you with all joy and peace as you trust in Him, so that you may overflow with hope by the power of the Holy Spirit.

- The presence of God will bring life to your dead body or any dead situation. Romans 8:11 says: The Spirit of God, who raised Jesus from the dead, lives in you. And just as God raised Christ Jesus from the dead, He will give life to your mortal bodies by this same Spirit living within you.

- The presence of God causes His light to shine upon you when you obey His commandments. (Isaiah 60:1; Psalm 31:16; Numbers 6:24-26; John 1:5; Psalm 37:5-6).

- The presence of God makes you enjoy divine favour. (Psalm 5:12; Psalm 30:5).

It is the presence of God Elohiym you carry that would help you to prevail in every battle. So, seek to remain in His presence.

All these are blessings you enjoy when you carry the presence of Adonai by obeying His commandments.

Psalm 91:1-16 says: He who dwells in the secret place of the Most High shall abide under the shadow of the Almighty. I will say of the LORD, "He is my fortress; My God, in Him I will trust." Surely, He shall deliver you from the snare of the fowler and from the perilous pestilence. He shall cover you with His feathers, and under His wings you shall take refuge. His truth shall be your shield and buckler.

You shall not be afraid of the terror by night, nor of the arrow that flies by day, nor of the destruction that lays waste at noonday. A thousand may fall at your right hand; But it shall not come near you. Only with your eyes shall you look and see the reward of the wicked. Because you have made the LORD, who is your refuge, even the Most High, your dwelling place, no evil shall befall you, nor shall any plague come near your dwelling; For He shall give His angels charge over you.

To keep you in all your ways. In their hands they shall bear you up, lest you dash your foot against a stone. You shall tread upon the lion and the cobra, The young lion and the serpent you shall trample underfoot. "Because you have set your love upon the LORD, therefore He will deliver you; He will you on high, because you have known His name. When you call upon Him, He will answer you, He will be with you in trouble. He will deliver you and honour you, with long life He will satisfy you, and show you His salvation."

The Almighty God Yahuah has assured us that when we abide in His divine presence, we will be protected from the arrows of the enemies, He will empower us to trample on the serpents and the scorpions and the roaring lions. So, we are not to be afraid when the powers of darkness come against us like a flood, because we know that the Spirit of God will raise a standard against them. His presence will make a way for you in the wilderness where there seems to be no way, just as He made a way for the Israelites to cross the Red Sea. So put all your trust in Christ the solid rock and nothing else.

Don't be like Lot's wife who turned her face from the Lord God and turned into a pillar of salt (Genesis 19:1-26). Rest in His presence always! Your joy can only be full when you dwell in the presence of the Almighty God. May the Almighty God grant you grace to abide in His presence, because you are about to give birth to that awaited miracle.

# CHAPTER SIX

# HONOUR AND RESPECT

Elohiym is a God of honour! He deserves our respect and honour at all times. It is an ordinance of God that has been put in place by Him for us to cultivate and let it become part of us. Our lifestyle has to reflect that we honour Him by living a life of faith, showing continuous gratitude, holiness, prayer, showing love to Him and others.

Revelation 5:13: says: Then I heard every creature in heaven and on earth and under the earth and on the sea, and all that is in them, saying: "To Him who sits on the throne and to the Lamb be praise and honour and glory and power, FOREVER AND EVER! AMEN.

The reason we honour, and respect the Almighty God Adonai is because of who He is and what He has done for humanity. It is impossible for us to fully comprehend the magnitude of God, His supremacy, His greatness! God humbled himself and came to this earth, born by a virgin into a poor family in a manger (Luke 1:30-33; 2:7) ;(cf. Isaiah 7:14). The God that created the entire world by His words (John 1:3).

The LORD of all Lords and the King of all kings lived a sinless human life during which He grew in wisdom, in stature, and favour with God and with man.

Philippians 2:6-9, Apostle Paul wrote: "Who, being in the form of God, did not consider it robbery to be equal with God, but made Himself of no reputation, taking the form of a bondservant, and coming in the likeness of men. And being found in appearance as a man, He humbled Himself and became obedient to the point of death, even the cross. Therefore God also has highly exalted Him and given Him the name which is far above every name, that at the name of Jesus Christ, every knee should bow, of those in heaven, and of those on earth, and of those under the earth, and that every tongue should confess that Jesus Christ is LORD, to the glory of God the Father.

Yahusha Ha-Mashiach, through His humility, obeyed the Father's commandment and because of that, Father God Yahuah honoured Him by giving Him a name that's above all other names, that at the mention of His name, all knees shall bow, and every tongue shall confess Him as LORD and God forever. This is huge. In Matthew 3:17, we read that immediately Yahusha was baptised, the Father God Yahuah publicly announced Yahusha to John the Baptist that this is the one He has honoured, this is the Messiah. "This is My beloved Son, in whom I am well pleased." (Matthew 3:17)

And the second time Father God Yahuah honoured and announced Ha-Mashiach was at the time of transfiguration in Matthew 17:1-5, when the voice of the Father said loudly to Peter, James and John his brother that "This is my beloved Son, in whom I am well pleased. Hear Him!" Why would God make this declaration? God made this declaration in order to honour Yahusha in front of His disciples so that they would know the truth, that He is the Messiah, the anointed one and not one of the Prophets. Because Peter had said to Yahusha in verse 4 when he saw Moses and Elias with Yahusha together, to let them build a temple for three of them; And after His disciples heard the declaration about the Messiah, they fell on their faces and were greatly afraid because they have come to know the truth of who Yahusha is (Matthew 17:6).

He is our God and Master! Therefore, we have to follow His footstep; if we want to walk with Him, then we have to submit totally to His leadership so that He can make us and empower us to do what we are assigned to do on this earth for His kingdom. When you know the truth of who Yahusha is, you will appreciate everything that He has done for you and for the whole world. To live in disobedience to His commandments will be a thing of the past because you know now that He owns your life. Until we honour Him, God the Father Yahuah cannot call us His beloved son or daughter. And until God Elohiym announces us as His sons and daughters, the kingdom of darkness cannot obey the word of God Elohiym in our mouth! The only way Satan and all the forces of darkness can obey the word of God when we declare them is when we are obedient to God's commandments and God has announced us as His sons or daughters, because honour is a law in the realm of the spirit.

## Difference between honour and dishonour

Anyone that dishonours a man cannot honour Elohiym! Because you can only honour God when you have learnt what honour is by honouring people that deserve es honour. And such a person cannot be honoured by God, he can only be honoured by worldly men because of his titles and achievements in life but not by God. Honour is a virtue. A man who doesn't have the virtue of honour cannot honour others. It is a character of the human spirit; a spirit that has been cultivated by the Holy Spirit.

It is expected that the virtue of honour should characterise our spirit. People who honour build others up, while people who dishonour tears others down. When someone is walking in dishonour, you will know that something fundamental is wrong with that person. That person will be selfish and full of pride; It has nothing to do with whom to honour, it's about who the person is.

Honour is a character, a character that is cultivated through process and training. When someone exhibits dishonour, it is a form of lack of training and processing. Someone who loves does not dishonour!

But lack of love brings dishonour. Behaviour that honours the Almighty God might not be an honour to the world, because the world does not honour God. The only way we can truly be blessed is when we honour God by keeping His commandments, by showing our respect to Him, because of who He is. Elohiym can only bless someone who honours and respects Him by keeping His commandments. The more we keep His commandments, the more we express our love for Him; that is when God Almighty will honour us.

1 Samuel 2:30b: But now the LORD God says: "Far be it from Me, for those who honour Me I will honour, and those who despise Me shall be lightly esteemed.

Psalms 91:14-15: says: "Because he has set his love upon Me, therefore I will deliver him; I will set him on high, because he has known My name, and I will answer him; I will be with him in trouble, I will deliver him and honour him."

Respect is reciprocal, so it is earned! Whatever you give out, you will get it back in return in one way or the other; and you cannot give what you don't have. If you don't honour and respect yourself, you cannot honour and respect God or a man. You cannot plant a fig tree and harvest olives in return nor can a grapevine bear fig. Whatever you sow is what you will harvest (James 3:11-12).

Luke 6:40 says: "A disciple is not above his teacher, but everyone who is perfectly trained will be like his teacher."

Galatians 6:7-9 says: Do not be deceived; God cannot be mocked. A man reaps what he sows. Whoever sows to please their flesh, from the flesh will reap destruction; whoever sows to please the Spirit will reap eternal life. Let us not become weary in doing good, for at the proper time we will reap a harvest if we do not give up. (NIV)

There are many things in God's kingdom that cannot function, if the law of honour has not been put in place. Blessings cannot be transferred except the law of honour is established. It will be difficult for any person to be blessed without the operation of honour, and many things can only be achieved through honour and respect, because honour is a law in the spirit and in God's kingdom. In 2 Kings 5:20-27: Gehazi, Elisha's servant, ended up a leprous man because he dishonoured God by going against his master's decision not to take gifts from Naaman.

There are so many consequences when we dishonour Elohiym our God and some of those consequences are afflictions, curses, reproaches, shame, and death. So, we have to watch how we act towards God and towards people. I have heard so many people using the name of our LORD and Saviour Yahusha in vain; Matthew 12:36-37: Jesus said, "But I tell you that men will give an account on the day of judgement for every careless word they have spoken. For by your words, you will be acquitted, and by your words you will be condemned." (BSB)

Through the course of history, there were people who caught God's attention in the Bible, God Almighty honoured them because they honoured Him by obeying His commandments. God is still the same; honour and majesty are before Him! He hasn't changed; if He did it to one, He will do it to others! When you see a man who always walks in the truth of the word of God; you will just know that this person loves and honours God. Whereas some believers, as soon as you come in contact with them, you will just know that this person does not love and honour God, because of their conduct.

When you see someone that God honours, whatever that person says comes to pass; Whereas when you see someone that God has rejected, whatever that person says never comes to pass. This is how you know a true child of God! This is the reason why keeping God's commandments is very important.

Hebrews 7:7 says: And without doubt the lesser is blessed by the greater.

## Men that honoured Elohiym

Genesis 12:11-20 is a story of Abram where he lied to Pharaoh that his wife, Sarai, was his sister. As Abram was about to enter Egypt, he said to his wife Sarai, "I know what a beautiful woman you are. When the Egyptians see you, they will say, 'This is his wife.' Then they will kill me but will let you live! Say you are my sister, so that I will be treated well for your sake and my life will be spared because of you." This is a man that feared Elohiym the Almighty God and obeyed His commandments to leave his father's house to a land that God wanted to give to him and his descendants. Now, he was afraid because of the kind of people that dwelled in the land, people that worshipped other gods and had no respect and honour for God and people. So as a stranger, he knew what they would do to him, so he lied that Sarai is his sister.

In verses 15-16, just as Abraham had thought, when Pharaoh's official saw Sarai, they praised her to Pharaoh, and she was taken into his palace to be his wife. Pharaoh then treated Abram so well for the sake of Sarai. Pharaoh gave Abram sheep and cattle, male and female donkeys, servants and camels, because of Sarai, Abram's wife, and Abram could not do anything because he was afraid of his life; God had to fight for him.

In verses 17-20, God got angry at Pharaoh and his household because of him taking Sarai as his wife, so He afflicted Pharaoh and his household with serious diseases. When Pharaoh found out the truth about Sarai that she was Abram's wife and not his sister, he was so furious and called Abram, "Why did you say, 'She is my sister,' so that I took her to be my wife? Now then, here is your wife. Take her and go!" Then Pharaoh gave orders about Abram to his men, and they sent him on his way, with his wife and everything he had.

You will think that because of what Abram did God will be angry at him and not at Pharaoh. The Almighty God Elohiym did not punish Abram for his sins, He knew that Abram through his obedience to His commandments got into this mess. God is a faithful God! He had promised Abram that He would bless him and his descendants if he left his father's house, who was an idol worshipper, to a land that He would show him, and that was what Abram did, it was in the act of obedience to God's commandments that he fell into committing this sin. So, Elohiym as a covenant-keeping God, did not turn away from His promise to Abram, but rather, he punished Pharaoh for taking Sarai as his wife by afflicting him and his entire household.

In verse 20, we read that when Pharaoh had found out the truth of Abram being the husband of Sarai, he sent Abram away not with an empty hand, but with everything he had acquired from Pharaoh and from the land. Abram left with so much wealth. When a man honours God, God turns his mistakes around to blessings. The Bible says in Romans 8:28: And we know that all things work together for good for those who love God, who are called according to His purpose (NET).

The Bible says in Genesis 20:1-18 that Abraham did the same thing he did to Pharaoh. He lied to Abimelech, king of Gerar, that Sarah, his wife, whose name was no longer Sarai, was his sister. The Almighty God Elohiym had changed both their names; Abram to Abraham and Sarai to Sarah, when God made a covenant with him in Genesis 17:3-5, 15. And Abimelech took Sarah to be his wife, and the LORD God Elohiym appeared to him in a dream and was very angry at him and asked him to return Sarah back to Abraham because she was his wife.

Abimelech had not gone near Sarah, and he responded to the LORD God Elohiym that it wasn't his fault and that he was innocent, that Abraham was the one to be blamed, that he did it with a clear conscience. Then God said to him in the dream, "Yes, I Know you did this with clear conscience, and so I have kept you from sinning against Me. That is why I did not let you touch her. Now return the man's wife, for he is a Prophet, and he will pray for you, and you will live. But if you do not return her, you and your entire household will surely die." (Genesis 20:6-8)

This is the second time Abraham lied about his wife being his sister because of fear that they would kill him if they knew that Sarah was his wife, and God still protected Abraham, his friend, and defended him and got angry instead with an innocent man, Abimelech. The next day, Abimelech rose up and called Abraham and confronted him for doing such a terrible thing; but Abraham responded in verses 11-12, "I said to myself, 'There is surely no fear of God in this place, and they will kill me because of my wife.' Besides, she really is my sister, the daughter of my father though not of my mother; and she became my wife.

Even though Abraham did an unspeakable thing, Elohiym still showed him respect and honoured him in the sight of Abimelech. Elohiym kept His covenant with His friend Abraham by defending him even though Abraham was the one at fault.

After Abraham had explained why he did what he did; Abimelech didn't get angry by killing Abraham, but instead, he blessed him with sheep, cattle, male and female slaves, and returned Sarah, his wife, to him. And Abimelech offered Abraham the opportunity to live in his land and he said to Sarah, "I am giving your brother a thousand shekels of silver. This is to cover the offence against you before all who are with you; you are completely vindicated" (Genesis 20:14-16).

What kind of respect and honour is this that the Almighty God has for Abraham? Abraham committed a crime, and he was liable to punishment, but rather God turned his anger on Abimelech and defended Abraham, and told Abimelech that Abraham is a Prophet, and he will pray for you so that you and your household would be healed.

When you obey Elohiym's commandments! He will cause you to enjoy His unmerited favour; and honour attracts favour! Abraham didn't know that God would favour and honour him this way. He never expected such a favour and honour from God even in his mistakes; Elohiym had to ordain him as a Prophet in the course of this. He had a relationship with God, he feared the Almighty God and honoured Him greatly, but he never knew that he was a Prophet until that day.

God made a lot of promises to him but there wasn't any time God had ordained Abraham to become a Prophet. The Almighty God Himself ordained

Abraham that day as a Prophet and asked Abimelech to meet Abraham to pray for him so that himself and his household would be healed from the reproach God had placed upon them, and for all the women in his household to conceive.

When a man honours God, no enemy can be able to withstand that person! God will make sure all your enemies are defeated and put to shame. To be honest with you, there's no enemy that can defeat me, I am not bragging, I am only telling you the truth. The enemies have tried several times to attack me, but they always fail and most of them have been destroyed. Why? Because I love and honour God. So, he honours me in return by fighting my battles for me.

Psalms 91:14-16 says: "Because he has set his love upon Me, therefore I will deliver him; I will set him on high, because he has known My name. He shall call upon Me, and I will answer him; I will be with him in trouble; I will deliver him and honour him. With long life I will satisfy him and show him My salvation."

Verses 17-18: Then Abraham prayed to God, and Elohiym healed Abimelech, his wife and his female slaves so they could have children again, for the LORD God had kept all the women in Abimelech's household from conceiving because of Abraham's wife Sarah. God Almighty never questioned Abraham for what he did, He never said Abraham why didn't you trust Me, you should have asked Me what to do? Why did you lie when you knew that I was behind you, after all I was the one who asked you to leave your father's house and go to a land which I would give to you and all your descendants to inherit forever.

Elohiym instead got angry at Abimelech and told him to meet His friend Abraham to pray for him so that himself and all the women in his household will conceive. And Abimelech in return blessed Abraham with many cattle, sheep, men and women slaves and a thousand shekels of silver. God Almighty made Abimelech to honour Abraham and his wife Sarah, instead of punishing him! Abraham became honoured and respected in the sight of Abimelech and his people rather than being shamed. Elohiym honoured Abraham and turned his sin and mistakes to blessings, because Abraham honoured and respected God by obeying His commandments.

God's ways are not man's ways! He said in His word that He will honour those who honour Him and will disdain those who despise Him (1 Samuel 2:30). Abraham instead of worshipping the idols of his father's house, chose to obey God, left his father's house not knowing where God was taking him to but humbled himself and followed God's instructions and directions. Many believers today are so stubborn that even when the Spirit of the LORD God is showing them signs, telling them what to do, where to go, they still remain where they are.

They might be living a lifestyle that doesn't honour Elohiym and Elohiym is telling them to repent, yet they still refuse; or they might be in a relationship that is not godly, and God is telling them to quit, and they still disobey. How can you be blessed? The Almighty God is telling you to follow His ways, and you insist on following your own ways, which will bring destruction and shame to you at the end. Everyone who disobeys God's commandments always regret it at the end! You can only be blessed by God Almighty when you follow God's instructions.

If Abraham had not responded to God's commandments to leave his father's house, he wouldn't have inherited the blessings for himself and for his descendants forever.

There's no obedience without sacrifice! Every act of obedience comes with sacrifice. Abraham sacrificed by leaving his father's house and following God's way, in return God honoured and blessed him abundantly and also his descendants. When you do what God requires of you, He will bless you; but when you decide to follow the system of the world and disobey God's commandments, then you are bringing dishonour to yourself.

Isaiah 1:19-20 says: If you are willing and obedient, you will eat the good things of the land; but if you resist and rebel, you will be devoured by the sword. For the mouth of the LORD has spoken. (NIV)

Proverbs 21:21 says: Whoever pursues righteousness and love finds life, prosperity and honour. (NIV)

On the morning of 15/06/24, my son asked me to do a sermon for him because he wouldn't be attending service the next day, which is a Sunday, because he is training with his new company. At first I wanted to get upset at him that he won't be able to attend Sunday service, but immediately the Holy Spirit asked me to do it, and immediately I calmed down and I responded to him that it's okay that I would do the sermon in the evening.

Then I asked the Holy Spirit what I should preach to him because I wasn't prepared; Normally it is me that would remind him that I will be sharing the word of God, but that fateful day, my son was the one that asked me if I would do a sermon for him. So, I asked the Holy Spirit for the message He wanted me to preach, and instantly He told me, "The Obedient Child." I said okay, but I was reluctant about the topic because I am not perfect as well to preach this kind of message; but the Holy Spirit kept troubling my heart until I agreed to preach it. So, I prayed for His wisdom and grace and that He should give me the right Scriptures, which He did, and I prepared the message.

In the evening, my family and I assembled in the living room, and I shared the message with them. After I had finished, they all complimented me, and said, "well done mum, that was really nice, we were all blessed by it." As I began thanking God for the message, the Holy Spirit immediately told me He wants me to write a book on this message, I said, "Holy Spirit wait a minute, this wasn't the original plan, how can I write a book when I don't have any idea or knowledge of writing a book, if it is to write a little message that I want to preach about, that's okay, but a book?" He responded and said, "yes, a book!" I said, "I don't think

I can, because I haven't written any book before and I really don't have any idea on how to write a book."

He responded again, "I want you to write a book on what you have just preached!" So, I asked him, "What is the topic?" Then He said, "Total obedience." And I told Him again that I am the wrong person to write a book because I am not qualified to write any book not to talk of this topic—Total obedience. Then He said to me, "You can do it!" So I prayed about it and I accepted to write it if He will be with me all through the journey, and He said yes; I asked Him about the chapters; He said "Don't worry, just follow My instructions and spend time in My presence, so I started praising Him and spending time in His presence. Before I knew it, He had given me all the chapters I needed for the book.

And so, I went to church the next sunday and met with my pastor after service, and I told him that I want to write a book, and the title is Total obedience. I asked him to agree with me in prayer, and that was how I started this journey. It wasn't an easy journey because I had no idea on how to write a book, but the Holy Spirit kept His promise, He was always there to give me the right Scriptures and explain it clearly to me. Everything written in this book was given to me by the Spirit of God Elohiym, the Scriptures, and how to write it. This is His book; it is not my idea to write a book! This is why I know that this book will be a blessing to this generation that has forgotten God. This is what He wants the whole world to know; That we have to be totally obedient to Him so that we can live a life of fulfilment and manifest His glory.

Most times, He will direct me to read a book in the Bible, and by the time I finish reading the book, I have gotten the messages for that chapter. And that was how I finished writing this book. Sometimes it was hard because some of the things He asked me to write, I was guilty of, so as I was writing, I was also repenting from all my sins and mistakes. For the Holy Spirit to ask me to write this book, that means, this is what the body of Christ is missing —total obedience! And I believe that whoever reads this book will never remain the same again.

You can see that when we surrender ourselves to the Almighty God; He turns our lives around for His glory. If I had refused to comply with what He wanted me to do, this book wouldn't have been written, and probably He would have used someone else to write this book. That would have been the end of my assignment, because when He tells you to do something and you rebel against Him, He will leave you alone. If I tell you the encounters that I have had with the Holy Spirit since writing this book, you will be shocked, and it's all because I obeyed.

Proverbs 22:4 says: Humility is the fear of the LORD God; its wages are riches and honour and life.

James 4:10 says: Humble yourselves before the LORD God Almighty, and He will lift you up. (NIV)

# Honour to the handmaiden

In 2 Kings 5:1-14: The story of Naaman is another story in the Bible that really intrigues me. Through this story, I have come to understand that no matter who you are, if you respect and honour God, He will use you to bring glory to His name. Naaman was a commander of the king of Syria. He was a great man in the sight of his master and highly regarded, because through him the LORD God Elohiym had given victory to Aram. He was a valiant soldier, but he had leprosy. There was a young girl from Israel that they captured, when they raided Israel, and she served Naaman's wife. In verse 3, when the slave girl found out that her master had leprosy, she said to her mistress, "If only my master would see the Prophet who is in Samaria, he would cure him of his leprosy!"

This slave girl was supposed to be outraged at her master and mistress but rather she showed them the love of God and humbled herself to serve them diligently. And because of her character, and the fear of God in her life, Naaman and his wife treated her with respect and honour. And that was the reason she was able to walk up to her mistress and tell her "If only my master would see the Prophet who is in Samaria, God would have used him to heal his leprosy."

She had seen the power of God in Elisha's life, and how Elohiym was using him to do great signs and wonders, and that was why she had the faith and boldness to tell her master and his wife about the God of Israel and His servant Elisha. Do you know what it meant for someone to have leprosy in those days? This was not just an ordinary man, this was the chief commander of the army of the king of Aram, who had won so many battles. Those who had leprosy in Biblical times were considered as the lowest in the society, they faced rejections and were considered as unclean people.

This was the person of Naaman, even though he had great titles and had achieved great success, he was still termed as unclean. So many people in the world has achieved great titles and wealth but because they don't have God in their life, they're termed as unclean, because the only way someone can be clean is when that person is born again, sin makes us unclean and it is when our sins has been washed away by the precious blood of Yahusha, we can be clean.

In verse 4, Naaman was so excited when she told him about the servant of God that God is using mightily to do miracles. And Naaman went to his master and told him what the slave girl from Israel had said. And the king replied and urgently asked him to go. Instead of the king dismissing Naaman for believing the words of a slave girl, he was rather pleased to hear the words of the slave girl which Naaman told him, and the king wrote a letter to the king of Israel immediately, asking for his help to heal Naaman from his leprosy (2 Kings 5:5-6).

Naaman, a commander of the chief of army, humbled himself, believed the words of the slave girl and went to his king, to tell him that the slave girl in his house told him that there is a Prophet in Israel that would heal him from his leprosy. The reason Naaman could believe the words of the slave girl was because she was God fearing and she had shown them love, and I believe she must have done other things in Naaman's house that were pleasing to him; that was why Naaman was able to trust and believe her words!

The reason many prominent men and women are suffering today is because they are so full of themselves, pride has kept them where they are today. It could be that the answer to their problem is in the hands of their house help, or their employee, but because of pride, they won't ask for help from them. Also, God would have used so many employees to bring their masters and their mistresses to Christ, but because of their wickedness and disobedience, God decided not to use them. Everyone who reads the Bible in the whole world will read what God did in Naaman's life using this slave girl.

Verse 7: As soon as the king of Israel read the letter, he tore his robes and said, "Am I God? Can I kill and bring back to life? Why does this fellow send someone to me to cure his leprosy? See how he is trying to pick a quarrel with me!" You can see that the king of Aram does not know the God of Elisha, so he wrote a letter to his fellow king, thinking that the king of Israel was the one who had power to heal. Many times, we think our problems can only be solved by people; yes, most times God uses people to solve our problems, but we don't have to put our trust in people. And if the King of Aram had gotten the right information, that it is the God of Elisha who heals, using His servant Elisha, he wouldn't have made the mistake of addressing the letter to the wrong person, the king of Israel.

He got the wrong information and acted on it. Many believers today have gotten the wrong message of the gospel, they think the gospel of Yahusha is about prosperity, so all their mindset is focused on these aspects. When they see a believer that doesn't have wealth, automatically they assume that that person is not loved and blessed by God. It is only when someone has acquired abundance of wealth and riches that the person is considered as blessed, which is wrong. This is the reason many preachers have sold their souls to the devil in order to get rich by preaching the gospel of prosperity without the message of repentance, which is the reason He came to this earth, died, was buried and resurrected. Their Christianity is based on material things that would perish one day. They are termed as fools!

Luke 12:15, Jesus speaks: "Watch out! Be on your guard against all kinds of greed; life does not consist in the abundance of possessions."

Matthew 6:19-21, Jesus speaks: "Do not store up for yourselves treasures on earth, where moths and vermin destroy, and where thieves break in and steal. But store up for yourselves treasures in heaven, where moths and vermin do not destroy, and break in and steal. For where your treasure is, there your heart will be also.

Verse 8: As soon as Elisha the man of God heard what the king of Israel did, he sent a message: "Why have you torn your robes? Send the man to me and he will know that there is a Prophet in Israel."

If Elisha did not know the LORD God of Israel and if he hadn't paid the price to become a watchman at the gate, do you think he would have the boldness to say openly to the king of Israel, "Why have you torn your robes? Have the man come to me and he will know that there is a Prophet in Israel." If we have men and women of God like Elisha in this generation, do you think millions of people both believers and non-believers will be in bondage today? Of course not! Many people want to operate in the power of God, but they don't want to pay the price. That is why they end up selling their souls to the devil in order to acquire power that is not real and finally end up in hell.

In verses 9-10, Naaman went with his horses and chariots and stopped at the door of Elisha's house. Elisha sent a messenger to Naaman to tell him: "Go, and wash yourself in the Jordan river, and your flesh will be restored, and you will be cleansed." First of all, before God can do anything with you, He will humble you, He cannot use you when you have pride. Many people are going through trials because God is trying to humble them; most trials that we face in life are not all from the enemies. When Elohiym wants to humble you, or wants to take you to the next level, and for you to bear fruit for His kingdom, He will prune you. This is not punishment!

Proverbs 29:23 says: Pride brings a person low, but the lowly in spirit gain honour.

But Naaman, because of pride, was angry and went away and said, "I thought that he would surely come out to me and stand and call on the name of the LORD his God, wave his hand over the spot and cure me of my leprosy. Are not Abana and Pharpar, the rivers of Damascus, better than all the waters of Israel? Couldn't I wash in them and be cleansed?" So, he turned and went off in rage (2 Kings 5:11-12)

The reason the Most High God Elohiym remembered Naaman was not because he was a humble man and had the fear of God, it was because of the slave girl in his house. He wasn't an Israelite, but a Syrian. And because the slave girl knew the God of Elisha, she was humble and God fearing, that was why she was able to confidently tell her mistress about the Prophet of God, Elisha, and what he could do.

Now instead of Naaman to humble himself to obey the Prophet and go to the Jordan river to wash himself and be cleansed, he got angry and walked away, because for him, the Jordan river is not as clean as the rivers in Damascus, the rivers in Damascus were far better than the Jordan river! For him people who live around the Jordan river are inferior to people who live in Damascus. So, he wanted Elisha to send him to Damascus instead of Jordan; he was so full of himself, and God had seen his pride and knew that the only way to humble Naaman was not allowing the Prophet to see him directly or give him any special treatment.

# Elohiym despises the person of pride

Many believers today have missed their blessings because of pride and anger! God tries to humble them through certain situations they go through; and because they are so selfish and full of pride, they get angry at God and say all sorts of things: "Why would God allow such things to happen to me?" "Why me?" Why not someone else? Pride! May God Almighty Elohiym forgive you and show mercy on you if you are one of such. Many people have lost so many opportunities because of pride, and they are regretting it till today. Except God shows mercy, many people will be miserable in life because they have lost their time of visitation.

If not that Elohiym is a merciful God, Naaman would have remained a leper; God had to intervene in the life of Naaman using the slave girl. A leper, a man who was unclean despite all his achievements and titles, an outcast, who was supposed to humble himself before God and His servant, was instead filled with pride. He would have missed his miracle if not for God's mercy.

As a commander of high reputation, he preconceived that Elisha, the man of God, will come out and greet him, and then wave his hands over him and pray for him and he will be healed. He thought he could command God's servant to do as he wanted, because he was used to commanding people! "Pride" is a very bad thing. God wanted to heal him from his leprosy, but he was complaining and deciding how to be healed. No appreciation, no gratitude to God that He was willing to give him the bread that belongs to the children of God (cf. Matthew 15:22-28). So many unbelievers in the world are enjoying the children's bread, not because they love God or keep God's commandments, but because of a child of God in their midst.

In verses 13-14, God had to intervene by using Naaman's servants to speak to him; "My father, if the Prophet had told you to do some great thing, would you not have done it? How much more, then, when he tells you, 'Wash and be cleansed'!" So, he was touched by the words of his servants and went down and dipped himself in the Jordan river seven times, as the man of God had told him, and his flesh was restored and became clean like that of a young boy. God had to intervene by making Naaman's servants to speak sense into his head to glorify His own name. Remember, Elisha dared Naaman to come to prove the existence of a man who represents God in Israel. Eventually, Naaman agreed to do what Elisha asked him to do by dipping himself into the Jordan river seven times and he was made whole.

Yahusha told a parable about two sons in Matthew 21:28-31; there was a man who had two sons. He went to the first and said, 'Son, go and work today in the vineyard.' "The son answered, 'I will not,' but later he changed his mind and went. Then the father went to the other son and said the same thing. He answered, 'I will, sir,' but he did not go. "Which of the two did what his father wanted?" "The first," they answered. Likewise, Naaman at first refused to do what he was told to do by the man of God, but after the intervention of his servants, he eventually obeyed and was made whole, (verse 15), after Naaman had been made whole, himself and all his attendants went back to the man of God. He then said, "Now I know that there is no God in all the world except in Israel, so please accept a gift from your servant."

This is the reason the Almighty God Elohiym chose to heal Naaman, for His name to be glorified. Whatever God does in our lives; it is for a purpose, for His name to be glorified, we get the blessings; He gets the glory. From that moment, Naaman made a vow that he will never bow down to any other gods except the God of Israel (2 Kings 5:17-18). God Almighty knows how to humble someone and bring honour and glory to His name. For God to honour us, we have to be totally obedient to His commandments.

Luke 4:27 says: "And many lepers were in Israel in the time of Elisha the Prophet, and none of them was cleansed except Naaman the Syrian." (NKJV)

When we do whatever He asks us to do, that is when our situation will change and His name will be glorified (cf. John 2:5). God used the slave girl from Israel to bring Naaman and all his households to Him! You have been a Christian all these while and you have never mentioned Jesus Christ to anyone, and you call yourself a child of Elohiym. Just imagine, they captured this girl and she became a slave in a strange land, she didn't get angry at Naaman for what he did to her and her people; rather she behaved her best, showing honour and respect to her mistress, and because of her good behaviour towards them, they treated her with respect and honoured her as well. When she told Naaman and his wife about the man of God, they quickly agreed and did just as she had told them.

Psalms 8:4-9 says: "What is man that You are mindful of him, And the son of man that You visited him? For You have made him a little lower than the angels, And You have crowned him with glory and honour. You have made him to have dominion over the works of Your hands; You have put all things under his feet, All sheep and oxen- Even the beasts of the field, The birds of the air, And the fish of the sea that pass through the paths of the seas. O LORD, our LORD, how excellent is Your name in all the earth!" (NKJV)

Today how many believers will behave the way this slave girl behaved? After being treated badly by their boss? And later, you now found out that your boss has been afflicted with a chronic disease; are you still going to behave your best as a child of God by humbling yourself and praying for your boss? And treat him with respect and love? Or you will be saying all kinds of ill things about your boss and be thanking God for avenging you of your enemy. Most believers will go and testify in the church that God has fought their battles for them; instead of showing love to their boss and praying for God to use the situation to glorify His name and preach Christ to their boss.

This is why it is hard for believers to win souls for Christ, because the person we are going to preach to has to see Christ in us. Therefore, we should be very careful in how we treat people because we are the light of the world, we are to shine our light and bring peace to everyone we meet. If we want to win souls for Christ; we should be like Him, honouring people, showing compassion and love towards people, instead of looking down on people, talking down on people, and criticising them especially in the household of God; we should pray for them! If the slave girl had talked down on Naaman, laughed at him, or spoken ill of him; she wouldn't have convinced him to meet with the man of God, Elisha, and he wouldn't have received his miracle, repented and worshipped God with his entire household!

1 Peter 2:12 says: "Having your conduct honourable among the gentiles, that when they speak against you as evildoers, they may, by your good works which they observe, glorify God on the day of visitation."

The slave girl brought honour to God and in return she was honoured, even though her name wasn't mentioned in the Bible, God recognised her, and it will be a memorial throughout history till Yahusha Adonai returns.

1 Peter 5:5-7 says: "Likewise you younger people, submit yourselves to your elders. Yes, all of you be submissive to one another, and be clothed with

humility, for 'God resists the proud, but gives grace to the humble.' Therefore, humble yourselves under the mighty hand of God, that He may exalt you in due time, casting all your care upon Him, for He cares for you."

## Who do we honour?

1. **Elohiym.** From the Scriptures, you will find out that God deserves to be honoured firstly in our lives: Exodus 20:1-5; Romans 12:1; Deuteronomy 5:6-10; Acts 5:29; John 14:21. Without love for God, it will be difficult to honour and respect Him. We should always honour and respect God with our lives, with all our heart, our soul, and our mind. We have to obey His commandments and put Him first in everything we do. Whatever thing you do without asking God for His opinion is a sin against Elohiym; before you do anything, you must pray about it first and let Him approve it first before going ahead to do it; that shows that you honour Him and He is your LORD and Master. Many believers never bother to ask God about what they intend to do! They just go ahead and do it and at the end everything collapses because they disobeyed God, and God cannot be mocked.

John 14:21 says: "He who has My commandments and keeps them, it is he who loves Me. And he who loves Me will be loved by My Father, and I will love him and manifest Myself to him."

The reason Jesus Christ could not do any miracle in his own town is because they dishonoured Him. They say is this not the carpenter's son? They looked down on Him and they missed their blessings and the time of their visitation (Mark 6:1-6).

> **2. Our Parents.** Every child is to obey and honour their parents, because it is a commandment from God. This is why it is very crucial for parents to teach their children how to be obedient to God. Any child that doesn't fear his or her parents, can never fear God. So, it is very important that parents train their children in the fear of God so that they would know how to honour their parents. (Exodus 20:12; cf. Matthew 19:19)

I know there are some parents that don't deserve to be honoured, but because it is God's commandments, we have to honour them and pray for God's will to be done in their lives. Many people today obey their teachers, their pastors, their leaders but never obey their parents. Such people will never be blessed by God. If you do not honour your parents, how can you honour God? Because if you honour God, you will honour your parents who God used to bring you into this world and has been taking care of you; no matter who they are and what they have done, you have to love them and honour them; because it is God's commandments. And this doesn't mean parents should maltreat or abuse their children; any parent who abuses their children has brought curse upon themselves.

Colossians 3:21 says: Fathers, do not provoke or irritate or exasperate your children (with demands that are trivial or unreasonable or humiliating or abusive; nor by favouritism or indifference; treat them tenderly with lovingkindness), so they will not lose heart and become discouraged or unmotivated (with their spirits broken) AMP.

Therefore, as a parent you have an important role in raising your children, teaching them the difference between right and wrong, and it is only when you honour God that you can be able to train your child up in the ways of the LORD God Almighty; and this is the only way your child can honour and respect you back.

Proverbs 22:6 says: Train up a child in the way he should go (teaching him to seek God's wisdom and will for his abilities and talents), Even when he is old, he will not depart from it. (AMP)

3. **Spiritual Leaders.** 1 Timothy 5:17-18 says: Let the elders who rule well be counted worthy of

double honour, especially those who labour in the word and doctrine.

1 Peter 5:2-4 says: "Shepherd the flock of God which is among you, serving as overseers, not by compulsion but willingly, not for dishonest gain but eagerly; nor as being lords over those entrusted to you, but being examples to the flock; and when the chief Shepherd appears, you will receive the crown of glory that does not fade away."

The reason why the obedient church leaders, the true ministers of Christ deserve double honour is because they are responsible for our spiritual growth. They watch over the congregation in prayers. They will give an account of the life of every member in their congregation that God has given them. God will hold them responsible if they fail to watch over the congregation. Because of the assignment given to them, they have to live a certain lifestyle of holiness to be able to stand before God in intercession. They face a lot of criticism, a lot of trials and temptation.

This is why we pray for God's grace and wisdom upon their life and their protection and also, for them to be focused and be obedient to God's will till the end. You should never be in a church where God is not honoured. And any leader or minister who does not honour and respect God and man, will never be honoured by God and by man. True honour comes from God, it is only when a leader honours God that God will honour such a minister. So many leaders in the body of Christ have stopped honouring God because they are now operating through another spirit; their assignment is to lead God's children astray. In fact, you should stay far away from any pastor or leader that doesn't honour and respect God.

Matthew 18:6 says: But whoever causes one who believe in Me to stumble and sin (by leading him away from My teaching), it would be better for him to have a heavy milestone (as large as one turned by a donkey) hung around his neck and to be drowned in the depth of the sea. (AMP)

4. **People In Authority.** 1 Timothy 2:1-2 says: First of all, then, I urge that petitions, prayers, intercessions, and thanksgivings be made for everyone, for kings and all those who are in authority, so that we may lead a tranquil and quiet life in all godliness and dignity. This is good, and it pleases God our Saviour, who wants everyone to be saved and to come to the knowledge of the truth. (cf. Romans 13:1-7)

The Bible makes special mention of praying for those in positions of authority. Such authority includes government officials, pastors, church elders, school boards, school principals, employers etc. We pray for our leaders because it's an instruction from God; and when we pray for our leaders, we bring the will of God to be done on this earth; we can only be at peace in the land we are living in when people that are in authority fear God and do His will. This is why God wants us to pray for them so that they would rule the people in the fear of the LORD Elohiym, for peace and holiness to be in the land. So, we have to pray for their salvation if we are uncertain that they know God; but whether our leaders are believers and followers of Jesus Christ or not, we should pray that God should guide them to do the right thing and follow all truth, and to protect them from the evil ones.

James 5:19-20 says: "Brethren, if anyone among you wanders from the truth, and someone turns him back, let him know that he who turns a sinner from the error of his way will save a soul from death and cover a multitude of sins."

1 Peter 2:17 says: Honour all people. Fear God. Honour the King.

Whoever walks in the love of Elohiym operates in honour. Let us all walk in love and honour one another, for this is the will of God for all men, so that we can work together in fulfilling God's will for our lives. May the Almighty God Elohiym bless you as you begin to honour God by keeping His commandments and treating people with love and respect.

# CHAPTER SEVEN

# FEARLESS

Fear is an unpleasant experience that can cause emotional distress which can result in body pains. Fear has a way of robbing us of our peace, joy and our walk with God when we allow it! It is a torment to the human soul, spirit and body, especially when we see and hear all the evil things happening around us and in the world. It might even be that you have lost a loved one and things seem not to be going in the direction you expected, and all these negative voices keep whispering in your ears that it is over. It might also be that you are going through some serious health challenges, that the doctors have told you there's no way out. Well, I have good news for you! It is not over until God says so.

As long as you abide by His word, He has the final say in every situation in your life! In three hundred and sixty-five places in the Bible, God has warned us not to be afraid; He wants us to trust Him and depend on His words completely! We are not alone; we live in Christ and He alone is our shield. As long as we have a relationship with Him, we know that He will take care of us and fight our battles for us.

When fear arises, fearless people don't let it linger! Our confidence in God and His word should always be the first thing to remember when we face any negative situation in life. God in His word has told us not to be afraid of the enemies, because our LORD Yahusha has already defeated the devil and all the powers of the kingdom of darkness. We are born of the Spirit of the Sovereign God. We are created in his image to be fearless so that we can represent Him here on earth. Therefore, we cannot be afraid of whatever battles we might face! Be it sickness or death; we will stand firm in His unfailing word! When challenges rise up against us to test our faith in Christ, we should stand boldly like David when he confronts Goliath: we cannot fear what the enemies can do unto us because we know whom we belong to, the Almighty God!

1 John 5:4-5 says: Whatever is born of God overcomes the world. And this is the victory that has overcome the world-our faith. Who is he who overcomes the world, but he who believes that Jesus Christ is the Son of God.

Psalm 118:6 says: "The LORD is on my side; I will not fear. What can man do to me?

The only one we are to fear is the Almighty God and the fear I am talking about is not because He is a wicked God, so we fear Him, absolutely not! We fear Him because of who He is, because He is our God and Father. He is the KING of all Kings and the LORD of all Lords, He is the ALPHA and OMEGA, the Creator of the whole universe. We fear Him alone and nothing else.

Colossians 2:15 says: "Having disarmed principalities and powers, He made a public spectacle of them, triumphing over them in it.

When you know this truth of the enemies being defeated totally, how can you still live in fear, or be afraid of anything? When you know the truth of a thing, it sets you free from the lies of the enemies. Truth overcomes all fear! If I knew the truth that all my bills had been paid for, would I still be worrying about paying my bills? Of Course I won't worry anymore! I will relax and be at peace. Likewise, when you come to know the truth that Jesus Christ has paid it all for you, you will relax your mind and be at peace.

The Almighty God is always by our side wherever we go; He will not forsake us nor leave us alone. He is a faithful God, and a loving Father, so don't be afraid of whatever you might be going through because He who has called you out from darkness and has brought you into His marvellous light will never abandon you in any situation you might be facing. He asked us to be strong and be courageous in the midst of trials and temptations. He said in His words that He is in us, and with us, to protect us from the weapons of the enemies.

Joshua 1:9 says: "Have I not commanded you? Be strong and of good courage; do not be afraid, nor be dismayed, for the Lord your God is with you wherever you go."

If we obey God's commandments and walk in love, there's no way we will be afraid of the arrows of the enemies. Elohiym is bigger than any power that's operating in any realm of darkness. The word of God in Philippians 2:10-11 says, that at the name of Yahusha Ha-Mashiach every knee should bow, of those in heaven, and of those on the earth, and of those under the earth, and that every tongue should confess that Yahusha Ha-Mashiach is LORD, to the glory of God the Father.

Every creation in the universe bows to Yahusha! He is the Head of all principalities and powers, and you dwell in Him and are complete in Him and seated with Him in the heavenly places (Colossians 2:10); it's like a woman when she is pregnant with a baby, is it the baby that would be worrying on how to be fed and be taken care of? Or it is the parent's responsibility to make sure that the baby is safe and well in the womb? Likewise, don't worry about anything that you might be going through that you are not in control of, relax in His hands! Because God is in control of your life if you are living for Him and Him alone.

Acts 17:28 says: "For in Him we live and move and have our being, as also some of your own poets have said, 'For we are also His offspring.'

We are operating from the authority of Yahusha Adonai, which is far above every principality, powers, and thrones! Elohiym has given us His authority which is far greater than the powers of Satan. Even though we are living on this earth, we are not of this world, so we do not operate from this earthly realm! We are operating through the power of the Holy Spirit that is in us, which is far above all the princes and rulers of darkness. The most amazing thing is that the Holy Spirit operates through us, because He lives in us, if we allow Him! Our body is His dwelling place so don't be afraid of any Satanic power that's coming against you in whatever form, rather be afraid of Him who can destroy both the body and soul in hell.

1 Corinthians 15:47-49 says: "The first man (Adam) is from the earth, earthly (made of dust); the second Man (Christ, the Lord) is from heaven, (cf. Genesis 2:7) As is the earthly man (the man of dust), so are those who are of earth; and as is the heavenly (Man), so are those who are of heaven. Just as we have borne the image of the earthly (the man of dust), we will also bear the image of the heavenly (the Man of heaven). AMP.

## Be bold as a lion

Lions are unique animals! These animals have always been considered as the symbol of bravery, courage, strength, fearlessness and ferocity. Lions are natural leaders who are focused on achieving their goals. Their roar can be heard from miles away! They are called the king of the beasts! They know who they are; the lion has full confidence in himself; no animal can oppress these animals. You cannot fear when you know that you are created in God's image; if an animal that is not created in the image of God, that doesn't carry the Spirit of God, is bold and fearless; how much more you that is created in the image of the Almighty God Elohiym and He dwells in you; be courageous and have full confidence in the LORD God Almighty! This is the only way you can grow spiritually.

Proverbs 28:1 says: "The wicked flee when no man pursueth; but the righteous are bold as a lion.

"If you build an army of 100 lions and their leader is a dog, in any fight, the lions will die like a dog. But if you build an army of 100 dogs and their leader is a lion, all dogs will fight like a lion." (Napoleon Bonaparte).

We are born in Christ to rule as kings and priests, we are naturally born as leaders and warriors! We carry the nature and character of Elohiym! We are created to act like Him, bold and fearless, yet very humble and merciful! Thus, we have to be conscious at all times of who we are in Christ, that His Spirit is in us, and we are His offspring because we are created in the likeness of Him (cf. Genesis 1:26-27). The reason many believers are afraid of the devil is because they don't know who they are in Christ, and that is because they are not taught the word of God! They don't have the word of God in them, so they don't have the revelation of who Christ is; this is the reason God said, "Do not let My words depart from your mouth, meditate on them day and night," because it is through the words of God you know that you can stand bold.

Joshua 1:8 says: "This book of the law shall not depart from your mouth, but you shall meditate on it day and night, that you may observe to do according to all that is written in it. For then you will make your way prosperous, and then you will have good success."

Jeremiah 1:10 says: See; "I have this day set you over the nations and over the kingdoms, to root out and pull down, to destroy and to throw down, to build and to plant."

Without knowing the word of Elohiym and abiding by them, we cannot live a fearless life! To pull down principalities and powers, we need to be fearless and bold, having faith in the word of God. If we abide in Him and He in us, it will be impossible for the enemies to harm us; yes, they will come against us, but they will never prevail against us. You were created to trample upon snakes and all the powers of darkness and absolutely nothing can harm you according to Luke 10:19; even though the mountains shake and be carried into the midst of the sea, you shouldn't be moved because He is in your midst.

Isaiah 54:17, says: "No weapon formed against you shall prosper, and every tongue which rises against you in judgement, you shall condemn. This is the heritage of the servants of the Lord God, and their righteousness is from Me," says the LORD God.

## Knowing the truth is what empowers you

The only way for us to live a victorious life is knowing the truth and living by it! Let's say, your earthly father is the king of a nation, will you be afraid of anyone trying to intimidate you? Of course not: because you are always conscious of who you are, even when you are just taking a walk along the street, you will be conscious of who you are as a prince or a princess. But the Bible said you are the child of the Most High God, the KING of all kings and the LORD of all Lords, all earthly kings and Lords bow to Him. That is your father, you are the child of the only true KING, so don't be afraid! Rejoice because this is huge; and this is what the Prophets and the Apostles knew that empowered them to do incredible things while they were on this earth. The truth you know will set you free!

Ephesians 2:10, says: "For we are His workmanship, created in Christ Jesus for good works, which God prepared beforehand, that we should walk in them.

We are created for greatness! We are not just some kind of creature that Elohiym created and put in this earth, we are created to reign here on earth as kings and priests, to have dominion over everything that God has created in this world; we are to take over! If you are living in fear? How can you take over? How can you rule over the affairs of this earth? How can you execute God's will to be done here on earth? We are His ambassadors, we are His sons and daughters, we are His brides, we are His battle axe, we are His body, representing Him here on earth, so relax in His presence! The God in you is bigger, greater, stronger than all the powers of darkness.

2 Timothy 1:7: says: "For God has not given us a spirit of fear, but of power and of love and of a sound mind."

Do you know what it meant for Moses to face Pharaoh after he had been in exile for forty years, in order to deliver the children of Israel who had lived in bondage in Egypt for four hundred and thirty years? God Almighty appeared to Moses in a burning bush and asked him to go back to the place he ran away from, because he killed an Egyptian, to the family who had raised him as their child that he betrayed, to tell Pharaoh that God said; "Let My people go so that they would serve Me." (Exodus 3:2-18); ( cf. Exodus 4:22-23).

It takes courage and fearlessness to stand in front of the king of Egypt and challenge him to release God's children so that they would serve Him; it takes boldness and faith to face Pharaoh that kept the children of God in slavery for years. But Moses put his confidence in God and went to confront his greatest fear Pharaoh the king of Egypt. When you read the whole story, you will find out how God displayed His power in the land of Egypt, how He destroyed all the first born of the Egyptians and brought plagues to the land that destroyed their cattle and their crops. God brought complete judgement on the Egyptians and delivered the children of Israel. The same way Elohiym told Moses that He has made him god over Pharaoh;

He is telling you in His word that He has made you god over all the powers of darkness and you are His, so don't be afraid of their faces.

Exodus 7:1 says: "And Yahuah said to Moses; "See, I have made you an Elohiym to Pharaoh, and Aaron your brother shall be your Prophet (CEPHER).

John 10:34: Yahusha answered them, "Is it not written in the writings, I said, Ye are Elohiym?"

Psalm 82:6a says: "I have said, Ye are elohiym; And all of you are children of El Elyon (CEPHER).

# Faith in the Almighty God makes you fearless

Before we can exercise our dominion and authority Yahusha Ha-Mashiach has given us, we need to trust Him completely and obey His word. If Moses didn't trust God completely, I don't think he would have had the boldness to confront Pharaoh to let God's people go! It is because Moses knew who he belonged to and had heard all the signs and wonders God had done in the lives of his ancestors; and also, his mother had told him about the story of his birth and so he knew that his Elohiym is the Supreme God amongst other gods, the Creator of heaven and earth.

So when God Almighty Elohiym appeared to him in the burning bush and asked him to go back to Egypt and to meet with Pharaoh to let His people go, he didn't disobey, he went with Aaron to Egypt as God has commanded them and they met with Pharaoh face to face and asked Pharaoh to let God's children go free so that they can serve Him (Exodus 3). When you go through the whole Bible, everyone God chose for an assignment, is always bold and fearless.

Moses saw an Egyptian man fighting an Israelite man, he killed the Egyptian man, even when he knew the consequences he would face when Pharaoh found out; but he still went ahead and killed the Egyptian man. This doesn't mean you should go and kill someone; please do not kill anyone, it is a big sin in the eyes of God, and you will be jailed for life. But it took boldness for him to do what he did! But if you don't know who you are in Christ, you can never exercise any authority over the devil! Because you will be filled with fear, and this is one of the major weapons the devil uses to attack the children of God Almighty Elohiym.

Mark 16:17-18 says: "These signs will follow those who believe, In My name they will cast out demons; they will speak with new tongues; they will take up serpents; and if they drink anything deadly, it will by no means hurt them; they will lay hands on the sick, and they will recover."

These signs can only follow those who know the only true God Elohiym, whose name is Yahusha Ha-Mashiach, who has conquered the kingdom of darkness and made a public show of them! Who is now seated at the right hand of the Father (Hebrews 10:12).

We are far above all principalities and powers! Because we are in Christ, we are the head and not the tail, we cannot be subdued by the enemies, because the enemies have been defeated long ago. You will always rejoice when you know this truth and even when the enemies rise up against you, you will not panic but rejoice.

## Fearless Daniel

Daniel was a man filled with wisdom, knowledge, understanding in all visions and dreams, because he feared and honoured God Almighty Elohiym. The Bible says he was a righteous man (Daniel 6). When Darius appointed Daniel as one of the heads of satraps and governors over the kingdom, Daniel decided to separate himself above the satraps and governors because an excellent spirit was in him. So, the satraps and governors then sought to find some charge or fault against him but found none, because Daniel was faithful. So, these men decided to find another way of charging Daniel, which is concerning the law of his God.

They ganged up against Daniel because they knew that Daniel would definitely be found guilty because of his obedience towards God. These evil men made a royal statute and made a firm decree and went to meet with king Darius and said to him to sign a law that had been put in place by all the administrators, and satraps, the counsellors, and advisors, and that whoever prayed to any other god or man for thirty days, would be cast into the lion's den. The king signed it and immediately it became a law in the land. When Daniel found out about it, he was troubled because he knew what would happen, he went home, and went straight to his upper room window, where everyone could see him, knelt down on his knees three times that same day, and prayed and gave thanks before Yahuah Elohiym, as was his custom since early days.

So these evil men when they saw Daniel praying and making supplication before God, went straight to the king and made a report against Daniel and said to the king, "Have you not signed a decree that every man who prays to any god or man within thirty days, except you, O king, shall be cast into the den of lions?" The king answered and said, "That is true, according to the law of the Medes and Persians, which does not alter" (Daniel 6:12). Then the evil men told the king that Daniel had violated the king's law and therefore should be cast into the lion's den according to the law.

The king was greatly displeased when he heard these words about Daniel because the king liked Daniel. The king tried with all his power to deliver Daniel but could not because a decree had been made which he himself had signed, so he could not reverse it again. Then the men said to the king, "Know, O king, that it is the law of the Medes and Persians that no decree or statute which the king establishes may be changed" (Daniel 6:15).

When the king knew that nothing could be done, he gave a command to cast Daniel into the lion's den, and the king spoke to Daniel, with encouraging words of faith saying, "Daniel, your God, whom you serve continually, He will deliver you" (verse 16). So, they locked up Daniel in the lion's den and laid a stone at the mouth of the den and the king sealed it with his own signet ring and with the signet of his lords, so that the purpose concerning Daniel might not be changed.

According to Scripture, that night the king was restless and could not sleep till the next morning, then the king rose up early in the morning to the den of lions. And as soon as he got to the den, the king cried out loudly calling out to Daniel, "Daniel, servant of the living God, has your God, whom you serve continually, delivered you from the lions?" And Daniel replied to the king with joyfulness, "O king, live forever! My God sent His angel and shut the lion's mouths, so that they have not hurt me, because I was found innocent before Him; and also, O king, I have done no wrong before you" (Daniel 6:20-22).

Wow this is huge, what a faith! This is what obedience to God's word brings, it brings total protection, provision, promotion, and honour. The king was exceedingly glad for Daniel, and commanded that they should bring him out of the den, and they brought Daniel out of the den and Daniel was completely vindicated! There was no injury found on him, because he was faithful to God, the God of Abraham, Isaac and Jacob, the Creator of the whole wide world. And the king commanded those men that plotted evil against Daniel be thrown into the lion's den, together with their children, and their wives, and the lions tore them to pieces. The king then made another decree in the land that everyone must fear and revere the God of Daniel alone, and Daniel prospered in the land (Daniel 6:25-28).

## Then King Darius wrote:

"To all peoples, nations, and languages that dwell in all the earth: Peace be multiplied to you. I make a decree that in every dominion of my kingdom men must tremble and fear before the God of Daniel. For He the living God, and steadfast forever; His kingdom is the one which shall not be destroyed, and His dominion shall endure to the end. He delivers and rescues, and He works signs and wonders in heaven and on earth, who has delivered Daniel from the power of the lions."

Isaiah 8:11-13 says: "For the LORD God spoke thus to me with His strong Hand upon me, and warned me not to walk in the way of these people, saying: "Do not call conspiracy all that these people call conspiracy, and do not fear what they fear, nor be in dread. But the LORD God of Hosts, Him you shall honour as Holy. Let Him be your fear and let Him be your dread."

Daniel knew exactly what they would do to him, and he still went to his upper room. Not only did he go to his upper room, but he opened the windows wide towards Jerusalem and prayed three times as he normally did. He didn't allow their threat to stop him from worshipping his God Adonai. He didn't give any excuses not to worship his God three times the way he used to. He was very bold and fearless to do what would've ended his life. I know that the Bible commands us to obey our leaders, but on one condition, if what they ask us to do is not against God's law; but if the leader asks us to stop worshipping our God, then we have to act as Daniel acted. Anything contrary to the word of God, we have to disobey it. We can only obey commands that would not go against the word of God. Any law that our leaders implement that's against God's word should not be honoured.

## Do we obey God's word or men's word?

Acts 5:28 says: The high priest asked the Apostles, "Did we not strictly command you not to teach in this name? And look, you have filled Jerusalem with your doctrine and intend to bring this Man's blood on us!"

The reason God Elohiym Yahusha commanded us to always pray for all our leaders is because of this reason. If we fail to pray for our leaders, then the devil will definitely influence them to put a law that is against the will and plans of God. We are to obey instructions from our leaders that don't contradict God's words. For instance, if our leaders ask us not to worship our God or call His name again, do we obey the commandment or we should be like Daniel and like the three Hebrew Men and say "NO." Definitely, we will not stop worshipping our God and stop calling His name; God Almighty honoured Daniel in the sight of king Darius, because Daniel honoured Him and had complete faith in Him.

Thus, God showed up, He demonstrated His power to king Darius and everyone in the land, by shutting the mouths of the lions from eating Daniel. The lions could not do what they were supposed to do because the One who created all things, including the lions was in control. How can you know this kind of God and be afraid of witches and wizards? It is because you don't have a relationship with God, you don't know his words, this is the reason you're being oppressed by the devil. Most people have bowed down to the devil and become his slave instead of becoming a king and a priest, a son and daughter to rule over the affairs of this earth.

Matthew 10:28 says: "And do not fear those who kill the body but cannot kill the soul. But rather fear Him who is able to destroy both soul and body in hell.

Who has the final say over this world and the things of this world? It is He who created everything! The entire world belongs to Yahusha Ha-Mashiach: He created all things and for Him all things were created (John 1:1-4). The devil cannot do anything to you if you are living for God! The devil can only touch those who disobey God, who dishonour His word, who have nothing to do with Him. But if you are born again and you are living for Him, rest assured that the devil is scared of you. Because of Daniel's obedience, King

Darius made a decree in that nation that everyone must worship the God of Daniel alone.

Do you know what this means, a king that used to worship idols, saw the mighty power of God, immediately repented and became born again. The reason most leaders of the nations have not repented is because they have not seen the mighty power of God. If they had seen what King Darius saw, all of our politicians and leaders would have repented. So, it is left for us to go back to our Elohiym and repent of all our sins and start abiding by His commandments so that God can do great and mighty things through us in this generation.

## Reason to rejoice always

The reason you should always rejoice when you come across diverse kinds of trials is because God wants to glorify His name in your life and through you! Therefore, you have to trust Him completely even though it looks as if it's impossible to come out from that situation. When you look at Daniel's situation in the lion's den, it looked so impossible for him to make it, even for a second, but God Almighty Adonai shut all the lion's mouths and kept Daniel safe till they brought him out the next day from the den.

Yahusha Elohiym wants you to trust him completely in that lion's den you are in now and believe that He is still the same God that delivered Daniel from the lion's den, that delivered the three Hebrew men from the fiery fire; He is still the same God that raised

Lazarus from the dead on the fourth day, He is still the same God that fed the multitude twice in separate miracles, the first miracle was with just five loaves of bread and two fishes, and the other miracle was with seven loaves and few fishes; He is still the same God that opened the blind eyes and the deaf ears; He is still the same God that parted the red sea for the Israelites to cross over; He is the same God and hasn't changed.

He is the Almighty God who has delivered you from the pit of hell and has brought you to His kingdom to sit with Him in the heavenly places. He is the same yesterday, today and forever, this is His attribute. So don't be afraid, put on a bold face and walk in confidence! Walk in the truth that you have received, Yahusha Ha-Mashiach, our salvation. Be fearless even though you are walking through the fire, be fearless even when the storm tries to drown you, be fearless even when you're in your darkest moment, because you're not alone!

Psalm 30:5 says: "For His anger endureth but a moment; In His favour is life; weeping may endure for a night, but joy cometh in the morning."

Isaiah 59:19-20 says: "So shall they fear the name of the LORD God Almighty from the west, and His glory from the rising of the sun. When the enemy shall come in like a flood, the Spirit of the Lord God shall lift up a standard against him."

## Uncompromising faith

Acts 5:28 says: The high priest asked the Apostles, "Did we not strictly command you not to teach in this name? And look, you have filled Jerusalem with your doctrine and intend to bring this Man's blood on us!"

Who can fight with the Creator of the universe, Elohiym Yahuah, and win? In Acts 5:17-41, the Apostles were arrested and put into prison by the high priests because they were preaching in the name of Yahusha Ha-Mashiach and winning multitudes to Him; but during the night, the angel of the LORD Elohiym came and released them from the prison and asked them to go back to the temple and preach in the name of Yahusha Ha-Mashiach; these men should have been so frightened and backed out but rather they were filled with boldness and quickly went straight to the temple and continued preaching in the name of Yahusha Ha-Mashiach.

When the high priest found out that they were no longer in the prison but rather preaching in the temple in the name of Elohiym Yahusha, they were perplexed and outraged, and the high priest called them and strictly warned them never to preach again in the name of Yahusha Ha-Mashiach. But the Apostles filled with the Holy Spirit answered them in verse 29 "We must obey God rather than men." How many preachers today in the world can boldly say we must preach the truth and stand by the truth rather than pleasing men? This is the reason the church has not seen revival.

And when the high priest wanted to kill them because of the response the Apostles gave them, immediately a Pharisee named Gamaliel, stood up and intervened and said to the high priest in verses 38-39: "So in the present case I tell you, keep away from these men and let them alone, for if this plan or this undertaking is of man, it will fail; but if it is of God, you will not be able to overthrow them. You might even be found opposing God!"

And as soon as Gamaliel said these words the high priests let them go. If the Apostles were not bold enough to face these religious leaders, they would have ended up compromising and stopped preaching in the name of Yahusha; Matthew 22:14 says: "For many are called, but few are chosen." Why? Because many have compromised! That is why you see most ministers of the gospel living in fear, going about with bodyguards and calling themselves a witness of Jesus Christ. How? How many bodyguards did Jesus have when He was on earth? How many did the Apostles have? None! So, for any preacher to be going about with bodyguards that are unable to protect you, only means that that person does not know God and does not carry His presence.

2 Timothy 2:13 says: If we are faithless, He remains faithful!

It is the level of your understanding of the word of God that strengthens your faith, and the level of your faith determines the level of your boldness when you face challenges! That is why God Almighty allows us to go through challenges in order to build our faith. If you believe in Adonai, then have faith in His words completely; He has given you His power and authority over all the powers of darkness to cast them out and silence them and nothing shall by any means harm you.

Zechariah 4:6-7 says: "This is the word of the LORD God Almighty to Zerubbabel; 'Not by might nor by power, but by My Spirit,' says the Lord God of Hosts. Who are you, O great mountain? Before Zerubbabel you shall become a plain! And he shall bring forth the capstone with shouts of "Grace, grace to it!"

Every mountain standing before you has already been levelled to the ground; so, stop yielding yourself to fear; rather have complete faith in Christ the solid rock that can never be shaken.

Psalm 27:1-6 says: "The LORD God is my light and my salvation; whom shall I fear? The LORD God is the strength of my life; of whom shall I be afraid? When the wicked came against me to eat up my flesh, my enemies and foes, they stumbled and fell. Though an army may encamp against me, my heart shall not fear; Though war may rise against me, in this I will be confident. One thing I have desired of the Almighty God, that will I seek; That I may dwell in the house of the LORD God all the days of my life, to behold the beauty of the LORD God; And to inquire in His temple.

For in the time of trouble He shall hide me in His pavilion; In the secret place of His tabernacle, He shall hide me; He shall set me high upon a rock. And now my head shall be lifted up above my enemies all around me; Therefore, I will offer sacrifices of joy in His tabernacle; I will sing, yes, I will sing praises to the LORD God Almighty."

We are the light of the world! When we walk in faith, our light shines; this is why we do not walk by sight but by faith! The lions know who he is in the jungle, no kind of beast threatens him, and no beast dares come close to the lion to challenge him; the One who created the lion is inside of you and you're afraid. As believers, we are to put on the whole armour of God, be ready at all seasons, ready to stand for the truth even when there are oppositions (cf. 2 Timothy 4:2).

2 Timothy 2:3-4 says: "You therefore must endure hardship as a good soldier of Jesus Christ. No one engaged in warfare entangles himself with the affairs of this life, that he may please Him who enlisted him as a soldier.

2 Timothy 1:7 says: For God has not given us the spirit of fear but of power and of love and of a sound mind.

A good soldier is very courageous and brave! They are trained for any battle; they are fearless; likewise, you are a soldier for the kingdom of God, the Holy Spirit is training you for any kind of battle that would come your way. So, you cannot surrender now! You are not a dog that goes back to its vomit, you are a son of the Most High God Elohiym, a warrior in Christ! So, keep fighting the good fight of faith till your mission here on this earth is over.

2 Timothy 4:7-8 says: I have fought the good fight; I have kept the faith. Henceforth there is laid up for me the crown of righteousness, which the LORD, the righteous judge, will award to me on that day, and not only me but also to all who have loved His appearing.

Remember you are not alone! Don't be afraid, "Those who are with us are more than those who are against us." 2 Kings 6:16.

## All powers are His

All powers in heaven and on earth belong to God Adonai! No one can be able to pluck you out from His mighty powerful hands as long as you are obeying His commandments. He is your shield and your defender! He can never lose a battle! He is the LORD of Hosts, the Mighty Man in battle! So, relax and be glad that you belong to Him who alone has the power and authority to do anything that He wishes, and no one can ever challenge Him. Let your heart rejoice and your flesh rest in hope! Because He will not abandon you in that situation.

Apostle Paul was fearless and was bold to face whatever would come his way, even unto death because he knew who he was in Christ; He had walked faithfully with the Holy Spirit, so he wasn't afraid at all to face any persecution. Even when the Holy Spirit had revealed it to him that he was going to face persecution in Jerusalem, he still went regardless of what might happen to him.

Acts 20:22-24, Paul speaks: And see, now I go bound in the spirit to Jerusalem, not knowing the things that will happen to me there, except that the Holy Spirit testifies in every city, saying that chains and tribulations await me. But none of these things move me; nor do I count my life dear to myself, so that I may finish my race with joy, and the ministry which I received from the Lord God Jesus Christ, to testify to the gospel of the grace of God.

Psalm 104:4 says: "Who makes His angels spirits, His ministers a flame of fire."

The Apostles of Yahusha were martyred for the gospel except John who died a natural death but suffered greatly for the gospel! They did not count their lives as dear to them; all they wanted was to preach the gospel which our LORD and Saviour Yahusha called them to preach. They counted it all joy that they were worthy to be persecuted and die for the sake of the gospel. Today, how many believers will count it all joy when they face tribulation? Is it not these same false preachers who have turned the name of our precious Saviour into a money-making machine? That is why you will see them so afraid; they cannot go out without security guards. Because they know they have no protection from God!

Psalm 104:26: "There the ships sail about; There is that leviathan which you have made to play there."

Don't let the devil play with your destiny; wake up and say, "enough is enough, Satan get thee behind me!" You are a threat to the kingdom of darkness! Let the Spirit of God Almighty Elohiym in you roar out and put to silence any devil that would want to challenge your God. Say to the powers of darkness, "I am not your slave!" You are the battle axe of the King of kings and the LORD of Lords. He is your strength! Have complete confidence in Him!

Mark 16:17-18 Jesus said: "And these signs will follow those who believe: In My name they will cast out demons; they will speak with new tongues; they will take up serpents; and if they drink anything deadly, it will by no means hurt them; they will lay hands on the sick, and they will recover."

Psalm 112:5-8 says: "A good man deals graciously and lends; He will guide his affairs with discretion. Surely, he will never be shaken; The righteous will be in everlasting remembrance. He will not be afraid of the evil tidings; His heart is steadfast, trusting in the LORD. His heart is established; He will not be afraid, until he sees his desire upon his enemies." (NKJV)

# Study to be approved by the Almighty God

As long as you remain in Christ, the enemies are afraid of you! The reason why the body of Christ is oppressed by the enemies is because of ignorance. So many believers have opened so many doors for the enemies to come into their lives and afflict them because of lack of knowledge; God said, "My people perish for lack of knowledge" (Hosea 4:6). Seek God with all your heart and have knowledge of who Christ is; in which you will be able to stand against the arrows of the enemies. Search Him as you would search for hidden treasures! It is the knowledge of God you have that will enable you to obey His words and stand strong in the storm. Without the full knowledge of Christ, you will always be a victim of the devil!

Proverbs 2:4-5 says: If you seek her as for hidden treasures; then you will understand the fear of the Lord God; And find the knowledge of God. For the LORD God gives wisdom; From His mouth comes knowledge and understanding.

If you are a follower of the truth, you shouldn't be afraid of anything that the enemies would throw at you. Have a clear conscience! You are a child of the Most High God, you believe in Him, so the devil cannot defeat you, so stand steadfast in the faith! Those that know their God cannot be put to shame! So have a bold confidence in His words and rejoice in Him always because you're more than a conqueror. Even when things seem to be tough, we will not be afraid, we will put all our trust in Christ alone.

"Patience includes perseverance - the ability to bear up under weariness, strain, and persecution when doing the work of the LORD." We may face struggles while serving Him, but when we trust Him through those trials, we can claim victory in Jesus through perseverance. (Billy Graham).

I see joy all around you my brothers and sisters in Christ. So be bold and wait upon the LORD God Almighty.

# CHAPTER EIGHT

# GOD'S BEST FRIEND

From the onset, it was Elohiym's idea to have a relationship with us, for us to be His friend! That was the reason He made man in His image according to His likeness (Genesis 1:26). Everything else created, God spoke them into existence, but when He had to create man, He formed man with His hands, in His image, according to His likeness and gave man His Spirit so that we can have a relationship with Him. Man was made special and different from the other creations of God (Genesis 2:7).

Before Adam sinned, Elohiym had a perfect relationship with him, they were friends; He visited Adam every day to have fellowship with him. And as Adam continued to spend time in God's presence in the garden of Eden, Elohiym then created a woman to be his wife and Adam called her Eve. Elohiym and Adam had a very good relationship until both Adam and his wife, Eve, sinned against God by disobeying His commandment not to eat from the tree of knowledge of good and evil (Genesis 2:16-17).

Therefore, as they disobeyed His commandment, Elohiym drove them out of His presence and out of the garden of Eden, and that was how man was separated from God's presence. According to Scriptures, all men became sinners through Adam and Eve's sin! Yahusha

Elohiym now came and restored it back by paying the price for our sins through His death, because that was the only way to reconcile us back to our Father God Yahuah (Romans 5:12-19).

Romans 6:23 says: "For the wages of sin is death, but the gift of God is eternal life in Christ Jesus our Lord.

John 3:16 says: "For God so loved the world, that He gave His only Son, that whoever believes in Him should not perish but have eternal life.

It is His love for humans that made Him come to this earth to die for all humanity in order to reconcile us back to our Father God Yahuah so that we can have a relationship with Him and become His friend. And He gave us a condition that if we want to be in a relationship with Him, and be His friends, then we must obey His commandments.

In John 15:12-15, Jesus speaks: "This is My commandment, that you love one another as I have loved you. Greater love has no one than this, that someone lays down His life for His friends. You are My friends if you do what I command you. No longer do I call you servants, for the servant does not know what his master is doing; but I have called you friends, for all that I have heard from My Father I have made known to you.

Psalm 25:14 says: The friendship of the LORD God is for those who fear Him, and He makes known to them His covenant.

## Our relationship with God is so important

Why is our relationship so important to the Almighty God Adonai? Well, if we don't have a relationship with our Father God and Saviour, we would not be able to connect with Him to fellowship with Him in His presence. We would not be able to communicate with Him through prayers and worship; it's through our relationship with Him that we can boldly go into His presence and worship Him. It's through our relationship with Him we can be able to hear His voice clearer and obey His instructions! Someone who doesn't have any relationship with God cannot obey His commandments. It's only through our relationship with Him that we can hear His voice and differentiate it from the enemy's voice!

As parents, we all want to have a good relationship with our children, but some parents don't. When there's a good relationship between a parent and the child, both parties are happy. The child feels safe, loved, and accepted, and as a result, the child will grow up to be happy, confident, independent, respectful and be obedient to their parents and their elders. This can only happen when there's trust, good communication, respect, and enjoyment of time spent together. Likewise, when you see children that don't have a good relationship with their parents, they lack respect and honour. They usually turn out to have negative behaviours, low self-esteem, they feel abandoned and mostly abusive.

The same way, when we are in a good relationship with our LORD Yahusha Ha-Mashiach, our lives become meaningful, and that is how we can fulfil our purposes on earth. The Almighty God Adonai always wants to have a relationship with us, but it is humans that are separating themselves from their maker. They blame God for all the evil things that are happening to them and in the world! They don't want to take responsibility that the reason things are not working the way it should be is because they have failed to do the right thing, to honour and respect God by keeping His rules, which will bring peace to the land and to everyone.

Jeremiah 32:38 says: "And they shall be My people, and I will be their God".

James 4:8 says: Draw near to God, and He will draw near to you. Cleanse your hands, you sinners, and purify your hearts, you double-minded.

The Almighty God Elohiym wants us to draw nearer to Him by spending quality time knowing Him through His word. This is the only way we would build our relationship with Him and become His best friends. If the children of the devil can do whatever it takes to please their father Satan; how much we that are children of Elohiym, the Creator of all things including the devil. So, we should draw closer to Him every day by spending time in His presence studying the Scriptures and meditating on them.

To become God's friend is what every believer should strive for! So, make up your mind and start the journey with Him. And I believe this is what Elohiym has been waiting for; He is knocking at the door of your heart; so, open it so that He can come in and transform your life just as He did in my life. Walk with Him in total obedience, this is the only way to be His friend.

## Doing His will makes us His friend

In the Old Testament, it's recorded that Abraham and Moses were acclaimed servants of God who He called His friends openly. In the case of Moses, the Bible says: "The LORD God would speak to Moses face to face, as a man speaks with his friend" (Exodus 33:11). It doesn't mean that other great servants of God mentioned in the Bible were not God's friends, it only means that the Bible didn't explicitly mention them as His friends even though they all had a good relationship with Him. For instance, God mentioned David as a man after His heart (1 Samuel 13:14; cf. Psalm 89:20-37); and He made an everlasting covenant with him and his descendants.

And it was through David's lineage that our LORD and Saviour Yahusha Ha-Mashiach came from. Though all the great Prophets in the Bible were not mentioned directly as God's friends, they were still His friends. In the New Testament, Jesus Christ specifically mentioned Lazarus as His friend when Lazarus died; and the interesting thing is that Jesus Christ made an open invitation, everyone who keeps His commandments will be His friend. Thus, we ought to walk obediently in His commandments so as to become His friend.

In John 15:12-15, Jesus speaks: "This is My commandment, that you love one another as I have loved you. Greater love has no one than this, that someone lays down His life for His friends. You are My friends if you do what I command you. No longer do I call you servants, for the servant does not know what his master is doing; but I have called you friends, for all that I have heard from My Father I have made known to you.

The moment you are born again, don't remain lukewarm; eat His words the same way you're eating food and keep His commandments. Many believers think it's only pastors that have a relationship with God, so God can only answer their prayers; well, It's because of the way some pastors preached; they make you believe that God can only answer your prayers when they pray for you, and whatever thing they say, is what God will do; but it's a lie, God wants all His children to communicate with Him directly, and not through any middle man. Jesus Christ is our middleman; we all pray through the name of Yahusha, and I know every prayer that is prayed by faith and from a sincere heart, God answers.

Every child of God has access to go into God's presence and talk to Him (Hebrews 4:16). And don't think it's only when God starts to do miracles through you, that you become His friend, "No." As far as you're living your life for Christ and following His instructions, you are His friend. After all Abraham didn't do any miracle or signs and wonders, yet God called him "His friend." Lazarus didn't do any miracle or signs and wonders, yet Jesus called him "His friend." Lazarus and his sisters were Jesus' closest friends, and He used to visit them, and it was Lazarus' sister, Mary who poured perfume on Him and wiped His feet with her hair.

The Bible said when Lazarus lay sick his sister Mary sent a message to Jesus saying "LORD, the one you love is sick." (John 11:1-4).

John 11:11 recorded that Jesus deliberately stayed for an extra four days till Lazarus was dead before He told His disciples that "Our friend Lazarus has fallen asleep; but I am going there to wake Him up."

Jesus called Lazarus His friend, why? Because Lazarus and his sisters were faithful to Him, they trusted Him, they loved Him. Even when Jesus arrived at Bethany where Lazarus lived, the Bible said in John 11:35, that "Jesus wept." Now the reason why Jesus wept was not because He couldn't bring back Lazarus from death? He wept because He saw Mary and Martha and all the Jews weeping; He was touched by it and was deeply moved in His Spirit and was troubled, because He had compassion on them.

Secondly, He was troubled because of their unbelief and lack of understanding. Earlier on, He had told Martha that her brother will rise again. And Martha answered Him, "I know that he will rise again in the resurrection on the last day." But Jesus was not referring to the last day but what will happen at that instant. So, he further said: "I am the resurrection and the life. Whoever believes in Me, though he dies, yet shall he live, and everyone who lives and believes in Me shall never die. Do you believe this?" And she replied to Him and said "Yes, LORD; I believe that you are the Christ, the Son of the God, who is to come into the world." (John 11:23-27).

Yes! She believed in Him that He is the Son of God, yet she couldn't believe that He was able to raise her brother from the dead on that day. But it was Jesus who deliberately waited for His friend Lazarus to die so that they may all believe, including His disciples. So, when Lazarus became sick, He purposely waited for him to die so that he would raise him up for His name to be glorified (verses 4, 14-15). As far as Jesus was concerned, His friend Lazarus was sleeping and that was why He didn't bother coming immediately when He heard the news that Lazarus was sick.

And in John 11:41-46, it is written that Jesus went to the tomb where Lazarus was buried and He raised him up, and in verse 45, the Bible says, many Jews therefore, who had come with Mary and had seen what He did, believed in Him. When you become a friend of

God, whatever things you might be going through is for His name to be glorified.

Hebrews 12:6 says: "For the Lord God disciplines the one He loves and chastises every son whom He receives."

Until His heart desires becomes your heart desires, He will not call you His friend. Do you know why God trusted Moses to deliver the children of Israel from Egypt? It was because Moses' heart desire was to see the children of Israel delivered from bondage, from the hands of their enemies, the Egyptians. Elohiym knew Moses loved his people just as He loved them; that was why, when he first saw one of the Egyptian men fighting a Hebrew man, he got so angry and killed the Egyptian man and buried him. And the next day he saw two Hebrew men fighting, he tried to speak to the man that was hitting the other, "Why are you hitting your fellow Hebrew?" And the man said to Moses, "Who made you a judge over us? Are you trying to kill me as you killed the Egyptian?" When Moses heard this saying, he became so afraid of what Pharaoh might do to him when he found out, so he fled to Midian and dwelled there (Exodus 2:11-15).

God saw that the heart of Moses was after His heart! Moses took a bold step by killing the Egyptian irrespective of the outcome, because he saw how much his people had been afflicted by the Egyptians. The Almighty God Elohiym heard the cries of His people and saw all that Pharaoh and his people were doing to the children of Israel, and He had compassion on them and sent Moses to deliver them from the hand of Pharaoh.

Romans 9:17 says: For the Scripture says to Pharaoh, "For this very purpose I have raised you up, that I might show My power in you, and that My name might be proclaimed in all the earth."

Jeremiah 17:10 says: "I the LORD God search the heart and test the mind, to give every man according to his ways, according to the fruit of his deeds." (ESV)

Psalms 25:14 says: The friendship of the LORD is for those who fear Him, and He makes known to them His covenant. (ESV)

## Reason why Elohiym called Abraham His friend

I believe before God spoke to Abraham to leave his father's house and go to a land where He will bless him and his seeds, He had already spoken to other people including Abraham's father, but they all disobeyed Him and continued to worship their gods. So when Elohiym spoke to Abraham to leave his father's house, Abraham didn't hesitate, he quickly obeyed and departed with all his households, So when God saw the faith of Abraham, He was pleased with him and that was the reason the Almighty God Elohiym called Abraham His friend!

If Abraham wasn't obedient to His commandments, God wouldn't have called him His friend (Genesis 12:1-9). Abraham served God faithfully even though God had not done what Abraham really needed, a child. Abraham continued to be faithful to God following His instructions regardless of his childlessness.

How many believers would have still been faithful to God without complaining to Yahusha of not granting their requests. Many believers would have stopped trusting and believing in God; they would've looked for alternatives, going to the devil for answers. But in Abraham's case, he was very humble and honoured God, serving Him with all humility, and offering sacrifices to Him. After the Almighty God Elohiym had tested Abraham in the first round and he passed, He proceeded to the second test. God finally gave Abraham his long-awaited miracle at the age of a hundred years (Genesis 21:1-5).

When Isaac had grown up; one day God asked Abraham to take Isaac and offer him as a burnt offering at the mountain of Moriah, wow! Many people would have said, "God this is not your voice; Satan I cast and bind you and all your demons." But Abraham trusted God and obeyed His commandments to sacrifice Isaac, this is huge! What a great faith (Genesis 22:1-19). The Bible said Abraham took Isaac and went to the mountain of Moriah where God Almighty had told him to offer Isaac as a burnt offering unto Him.

But as he was about to sacrifice Isaac, God immediately called Abraham and said: "Abraham,

Abraham!" And he said, "Here I am." He said, "Do not lay your hand on the boy or do anything to him, for now I know that you fear God, seeing you have not withheld your son whom you loved from me." And Elohiym told him to look up and he will see a ram; And Abraham lifted up his eyes and behold, there was a ram behind him and God asked him to sacrifice the ram instead of Isaac which Abraham did (Genesis 22:11-13).

Earlier, Isaac had asked his father, Abraham, "Where is the Lamb?" Abraham answered with a statement of faith: "God will provide Himself a lamb." And God undoubtedly did provide Himself a lamb." The Saviour of the whole world!

1 Peter 1:19-20 says: But with the precious blood of Christ, as of a lamb without blemish and without spot. He indeed was foreordained before the foundation of the world, but was manifest in these last times for you.

And the LORD God called to Abraham the second time from heaven and said: "By Myself I have sworn, says the LORD God Almighty, Because you have done this thing, and have not withheld your son, your only son, in blessing I will bless you, and multiplying I will multiply your descendants as the stars of the heaven and as the sand which is on the seashore; and your descendants shall possess the gate of their enemies. In your seed all the nations of the earth shall be blessed, because you have obeyed My voice (Genesis 22:15-18).

When the Almighty God Adonai saw the faith and loyalty of Abraham, his obedience to the point of sacrificing his son, Isaac, He was compelled to bless Abraham and his descendants beyond measure. Abraham demonstrated His love and obedience to God by not just leaving his father's house and being where God wants him to be but by wanting to offer Isaac his only beloved son to God. He did exactly what God had already done even before the foundation of the world which eventually took place at the cross for our redemption.

Revelation 13:8 says: Jesus Christ was "the Lamb slain from the foundation of the world.

You can now see clearly why the Almighty God Elohiym called Abraham His friend (cf. Isaiah 41:8). To the extent that when God wanted to destroy Sodom and Gomorrah because of the greatness of their sins, God discussed it with Abraham to get his opinion.

Genesis 18:17 says: And the LORD God said, "Shall I hide from Abraham what I am doing."

And if you read Genesis 18:17-33, you will see how Abraham started a dialogue with the Almighty God not to destroy the people for the sake of his nephew Lot and his family. And Abraham started by saying: "If there are fifty righteous within the city; would you still destroy the place and not spare it for the sake of the fifty righteous that were in the land? And Elohiym Yahuah responded by saying "If there are fifty righteous people, I will not destroy the land. And Abraham continued to make a demand for God not to destroy the land until Abraham came down to ten righteous people.

In verse 32, Abraham then said, "Let not the LORD be angry, and I will speak but once more: Suppose ten righteous people should be found there?" And God said, "I will not destroy it for the sake of ten." The Scriptures inform us that God eventually destroyed the people but spared Lot and his household because of the sake of His friend Abraham (Genesis 19:12-29). You see, when you are a friend of God, He will reveal things to you before it happens so that you can act immediately based on what He has shown you. Elohiym cannot hide any of His plans to those who obey His commandments. Lot and his household would have all perished if not for the sake of Abraham.

John 16:13 says: "However, When He, the Spirit of truth, has come, He will guide you into all truth; for He will not speak on His own authority, but whatever He hears He will speak; and He will tell you things to come."

It is very important for us to walk in accordance with God's commandments, that's the essence of us being His children. If we call Him our Father and God, then we ought to believe Him completely and walk in total obedience to His commandments. This is the only way we can become His friends (John 15:14).

James 2:23 wrote: And the Scripture was fulfilled that says, "Abraham believed God, and it was counted to him as righteousness," and he was called a friend of God.

Proverbs 22:11 says: "He who loves purity of heart and whose speech is gracious, will have the king as his friend."

When you read the story of Abraham and his friendship with the Almighty God, you can see that it was based on trust and obedience. The same thing with us as believers, for God Almighty to call any one of us His friend, we must lay down our will and accept His will for our lives and be willing to carry our cross and follow Him wherever He wants us to go. Every step Abraham took was ordered by God; he followed God obediently to the extent of almost sacrificing his beloved son, Isaac. Now the question is? Are you willing to give up whatever He is telling you to lay down and follow Him so that He can turn your life around for His glory? Or you're still holding on to your will?

## Total commitment to God is what makes you His friend

When Jesus Christ met His disciples at the start of His ministry, they were fishermen who later became His friends, except Judas Iscariot, who betrayed Him. On a certain day, Yahusha passed by the seashore and saw these men. He said to them, "Follow Me, and I will make you fishers of men;" they immediately left their nets on the boat and their father and followed Him. These men were skilled fishermen, this is what they've been doing all their lives, which they loved (Matthew 4:18-22).

These men did not question Him, the Bible said immediately, they left their nets in their boats and followed Him. They had no idea the outcome of their actions, they just believed Him completely and followed Him to wherever He went. They didn't know the details of what Jesus meant by "follow Me and I will make you fishers of men." All they knew at that moment was to trust this Jesus and follow Him; they went with Him everywhere and were obedient to Him throughout His ministry journey here on earth.

In John 21:1-14, the Bible tells us after Yahusha had appeared to His disciples the evening after His resurrection in John 20:19-29, Adonai appeared again to His disciples at the sea of Tiberias. His disciples went fishing all through the night and caught no fish, and when Yahusha stood on the shore, His disciples didn't recognise Him at first. But why didn't they recognise Him? After spending three and half years with Him; well, it's because He is no longer putting on the first body that carried all the sins of the world, As He resurrected, He resurrected with a new glorified body and that was why no one was able to recognise Him, until He revealed Himself to that person. And this is why most people don't know Him, even though they claim to know Him; because He has concealed His identity from them, because they refused to obey His commandments. And this is the reason they are so heartless with no conscience, using His name to do all sorts of evil and deceiving themselves.

Thus, Yahusha spoke to them and asked: "Friends, haven't you any fish?" And they answered Him, "No." So Jesus gave them an instruction on what to do and they did it and caught a multitude of fish. This same Yahusha that you called your Lord and Saviour is telling you to follow Him in total obedience of heart and stop living for yourself because He wants to make you fishers of men, and you're saying, "No I am not ready."

As soon as they saw the miracle of fish, that was when one of the disciples, John whom Jesus loved, said to Peter, "It is the Master! Our LORD Jesus Christ!" And immediately Simon Peter and the rest of His disciples brought the net ashore, and Jesus Christ offered them to have breakfast with Him which they did. Jesus Christ called them His friends because they were faithful and obedient to Him. In the book of Acts, we read the great signs and wonders God did through the Apostles.

Now Yahusha Ha-Mashiach is saying to you through His words, the same thing He said to His disciple, to follow Him and He will make them fishers of men; He is saying to you now, "Follow me, and I will turn your situation around for good." You have been toiling all these years, and have made no progress, it is time you quit and follow Jesus. And even if you are successful in your career, you will still not be fulfilled; there will always be an emptiness inside of you unless you totally surrender to the One who created you! Whose name is Yahusha Ha-Mashiach.

Psalm 127:1-2 says: Unless the LORD God builds the house, the builders labour in vain. Unless the LORD God watches over the city, the guards stand watch in vain. In vain you rise early and stay up late, toiling for food to eat-for he grants sleep to those He loves.

Psalm 128:1-2 says: "Blessed are all who fear the LORD God Almighty, who walk in obedience to Him. You will eat the fruit of your labour; blessings and prosperity will be yours."

Finally, brothers and sisters, let us all humble ourselves before our LORD God and Father Yahuah Elohiym and walk in total obedience so that we can enjoy our friendship with Him. We are His children and are called by His name; so let us be sober and walk faithfully to fulfil our purposes here on earth and at the end, we would be able to stand before our LORD Yahusha Ha-Mashiach, and He will tell us "Well done, good and faithful servant."

# CHAPTER NINE

# LIVING A LIFE OF FULFILMENT

Elohiym's plan from the beginning for everyone is to live a life of fulfilment that would bring glory and honour to His name. God has redeemed us so that we can have a glorious relationship with Him and live a life of fulfilment. In order for us to live a life of fulfilment on this earth, there are rules we must follow, which is to go back to our Maker in total obedience and surrender completely to Him. This is the reason Yahusha came to die for us, so that we can be restored back to our Father God and allow Him to make us become who He has made us to be, to live the kingdom life, the life of Christ! To have dominion over everything He had created on this earth.

We were made to live an extraordinary life in Christ! That is dwelling in His presence continuously; this was the kind of lives the Apostles lived and the Prophets in the Bible. Just as Mary, His earthly mother, carried Him for nine months; we are to carry His presence continuously as long as we are on this earth.

Acts 17:28b says: For in Him we live and move and have our being.

Isaiah 43:7 God said: "Everyone who is called by My name, whom I have created for My glory; I have formed him, yes, I have made him."

## Only when we are connected to Him can we be fulfilled

The heavens and the earth are His! He owns everything including you and me. For us to manifest His glory and live a life of fulfilment; we must be connected to Him and do His will. When the branches of an apple tree are connected to the tree, it will bear good fruits, but if the branches are disconnected from the tree; it will die. A blind man cannot lead another blind man because both of them will fall (Matthew 15:14). We need the One that created all things, who brought us to this world; who knows why He made us, to guide us so as not to fall into a pit.

John 15:4-5: Jesus said: "Abide in Me, and I in you. As the branch cannot bear fruit of itself, unless it abides in the vine, neither can you, unless you abide in Me. "I am the Vine, you are the branches, he who abides in Me, and I in him, bears much fruit; For without Me you can do nothing."

Psalms 24:1 says: The earth is the LORD's, and all its fullness, the world and those who dwell therein.

We were all made for a purpose, we all have assignments to fulfil on this earth. If we disconnect ourselves from the One who made us, we are disconnecting ourselves from our destiny. It is the level of our relationship with the Holy Spirit that determines the quality of fruit we would produce. A plane cannot fly itself unless there is a trained pilot to fly it to its destination! Likewise, you cannot fulfil your purpose and get to your final destination, except you allow God who is your Creator to be your pilot.

Having wealth, education, a high position in office, and living a good life is good! But if the Almighty God Elohiym is not in your life and your first priority, you are just wasting your time. Someone who is living according to God's commandments and does His will is the one that is living a life of fulfilment. Most people feel they are fulfilled in life simply because of their career, or the wealth they have acquired, and various achievements they have achieved in life! So, they refused to have anything to do with the One who created them and brought them to this world. Christ came and offered us the free gift of eternal life! But people rather chose to follow the path of death and to rebel against Him.

The plans God has for each one of us is huge! He created us to represent Him on this earth! We were sent. He said in His word, "Let Us make man in Our own image and after Our likeness" (Genesis 1:26), so that they can do incredible things that eyes haven't seen, nor ears heard! Therefore, allow Yahusha Elohiym to take you to your destiny. The church of Jesus Christ has suffered a lot because of ignorance, and it is time we wake up and start seeking Him diligently so that we can live a life of fulfilment.

We shouldn't be satisfied until God's will is done on this earth and in our lives! We should only be satisfied when we have seen the glory of God manifest in our lives and through us to the whole world. When the glory of God has covered the whole earth, that is when we can say, "Yes, it is done, I have seen the promises of God being fulfilled" (cf. Habakkuk 2:14).

There was a man who lived in Jerusalem named Simone, he was a devoted man, and he was patiently waiting for the day God's promise will come to pass; and the Holy Spirit had promised him that he would not see death till he had seen the Messiah. So, when Yahusha was born, the Holy Spirit revealed it to Simone, and he came to the temple; he saw Yahusha, and he carried Him in his hands and blessed Elohiym and said:

"Yahuah, now let your servant depart in peace, according to Your word: For my eyes have seen Your salvation, which you have prepared before the face of all people; A light to lighten the other nations, and the glory of your people Israel" Luke 2:25-32 (CEPHER).

Simone was obedient to Elohiym, and he had faith that he will not leave this earth till he sees the Messiah, and God honoured his wish. So, for us as believers to see the promises of God come to pass in our lives and this generation, we need to be totally obedient to Yahuah's commandments. If Simone wasn't devoted to Elohiym, Adonai wouldn't have kept him alive to see His promise to Israel and the entire nations. Simone lived to fulfil his purpose; his heart desires were not on material things that would perish, but to see the Messiah before he passed away, and that was what God granted him.

The reason this earth is filled with all kinds of immorality is because humans chose to live a life that is pleasing to themselves rather than God! They have tried for several decades to become God but rather they brought destruction to themselves. The world is suffering from what humans brought to themselves! The only way we can experience the tranquillity of Elohiym is when we all repent and connect back to our LORD Yahusha Ha-Mashiach. Everyone seems to be doing whatever looks good in their own eyes without putting into consideration the outcome of their actions! Whatever direction you look in this earth now, what you will see is immorality! It's a shame! God took His time to create humans, to give humans a great life on earth and eternity, but humans prefer death.

So many people are dead without fulfilling the assignments God Almighty gave them to fulfil! Today, many people are busy pursuing their own agenda, living a selfish life! God haters! Never acknowledging God in their lives; living a life without God who created them! And when they die, that's when they will realise, they've made the biggest mistake in their lives because they will stand before the Creator, Yahusha, and then they'll know that He is the Messiah whom they rejected.

# Human's responsibility over the earth

Psalm 115:16 says: The heaven, even the heavens, are the LORD's; But the earth He has given to the children of men.

Psalm 8:4-9 wrote: What is man that You are mindful of him, and the son of man that You visit him? For You have made him a little lower than the angels and have crowned him with glory and honour. You have made him to have dominion over the works of Your hands; You have put all things under his feet; All sheep and oxen- Even the beasts of the field, the birds of the air, and the fish of the sea that pass through the paths of the seas. O LORD, our LORD, how excellent is Your name in all the earth!

God Almighty Elohiym has given the earth to man and the moment God gave the earth to man; God exonerated himself from events that occur on this earth. The Most High God can only get involved when man invites Him to take total control! He cannot force Himself on man and whatever man does, because He has given man the free will to choose, man has to decide whether to allow God into their lives or not (cf. Genesis 1:26-30)

1 Corinthians 2:9: says: But as it is written, "Eye has not seen, nor ear heard, nor have entered into the heart of man the things which God has prepared for those who love Him."

Elohiym has greater plans for everyone who loves Him! He is telling you through His words, "See I have better plans for your life," in order for you to fulfil it, you have to surrender totally to Me and let Me lead and guide you." He created you and I and the entire world! The world belongs to Him (John 1:3). And if the entire world belongs to Him, how do you think you can live a life of fulfilment without Him being involved? Whatever we do on this earth, it has to be according to His will for our lives and not according to our will. Our LORD and Saviour Yahusha Elohiym Himself came to this earth not to fulfil His will but to fulfil the will of the Father Yahuah Elohiym. There is a reason you and I are here on this earth; there is a purpose for your life! You are not here by coincidence, you are not here just to fill the earth, you are here to do your heavenly Father's will and for His will to be fulfilled in your life.

In Hebrews 10:7, Jesus speaks: Then I said, "Behold! I have come in the volume of the book it is written of Me–To do Your will, O God."

## The reason people perish

We are all here to do the Father's will; Elohiym Yahuah, who has made each one of us, the only way you are exempted is when you are the one who created yourself; but if it is the Almighty God who has created the heavens and the earth, who made you and I, then you must surrender to Him totally so that He can lead and guide you on the path to take in order for you to live a life of fulfilment. If you think you don't need Him to be fulfilled in life, you are mistaken! You need Him here on earth and for eternity; He owns everything!

The worst thing is that many believers all over the world are still slaves to the devil because of ignorance! Many believers are suffering because they refuse to know the truth. They lack knowledge, wisdom and understanding! They are tossed to and fro with every doctrine and are now living in bondage instead of living a life of glory in the presence of God Almighty (Ephesians 4:14). We are the light of the world! Either our light is shining so bright, or darkness takes over. Whatever things we sow, that we shall reap. Thus, we have to be very careful of the way we live our lives.

Many people have dreams and expectations but can't fulfil them because of lack of revelation and direction, and they're now living a life of frustration and bitterness; they are filled with anger! Many people have committed suicide because they couldn't live the life of their dreams! Many are drug addicts because they've abandoned the truth and followed the path that leads to death; then they blame God and everyone for their failures.

Hosea 4:6a says: "My people are destroyed for lack of knowledge! Because you have rejected knowledge, I also will reject you from being priest for Me!"

## Believe and act

If you believe in Yahusha and you're not living for Him, you are still far from living a life of fulfilment. Because the Scripture says, "You believe that there is one God. You do well, even the demons believe and tremble" (James 2:19). It is only when you abide in His words, allow Him to guide you, and He becomes the captain of your life, then, you can boldly say "I am living a life of fulfilment! I am a child of the Most High God!" When we look unto Yahusha alone, the Author and Finisher of our faith, when He becomes our focus, our priority, our goal, His mind becomes our mind, His will becomes our will! His desires become our desires; this is when we are fulfilled (1 Corinthians 2:16).

To become His replica, we must do what He did on earth! For we know that the will of our LORD Yahusha and Father is for people to be saved. Until we make this our number one priority, we would not live a life of fulfilment on this earth, even though we are successful in our various careers and jobs. Although John the Baptist and the Apostle were martyred, except John who died a natural death, they all lived a life of fulfilment. They counted it all joy to be persecuted for Christ! They never saw this earth as their home, they were all looking forward to finishing what was assigned for them by God to accomplish, their focus was Heaven!

Philippians 3:20 says: But our citizenship is in Heaven, and we eagerly await a Saviour from there, the LORD Jesus Christ. (BSB)

Matthew 6:33: says: But seek first the kingdom of God and His righteousness, and all these things shall be added to you.

## Have the revelation of Christ

Philippians 3:10: Apostle Paul speaks: (For my determined purpose is) that I may know Him (that I may progressively become more deeply and intimately acquainted with Him, perceiving and recognizing and understanding the wonders of His person more strongly and more clearly), and that I may in that same way come to know the power outflowing from His resurrection (which it exerts over believers), and that I may so share His sufferings as to be continually transformed (in spirit into His likeness even) to His death, (in the hope). (AMPC)

When we have come to the full knowledge of Jesus Christ, that is when His glory will start manifesting in our lives. Someone that has the full knowledge and revelation of Jesus Christ cannot operate as an ordinary man; they are filled with the fullness of

Elohiym. Even when things don't go the way they have planned, they're not shaken. Because they are built on a firm foundation, the word of God; so, they will still be rejoicing! Their mind has been renewed, they can see clearly their purpose and walk in confidence, fulfilling purposes.

Ephesians 4:13 says: (That it might develop) until we all attain oneness in the faith and in the comprehension of the (full and accurate) knowledge of the son of God, that (we might arrive) at really mature manhood (the completeness of personality which is nothing less than the standard height of Christ's own perfection), the measure of the stature of the fullness of the Christ and the completeness found in Him. (AMPC)

## Bringing glory to His name

As believers, our focus should always be on Yahusha! If at the end of the day, what we are doing is not part of God's plans for our life, then we have wasted our lives here on earth (Isaiah 43:7). And how do we bring glory to His name? By doing what He has called each one of us to do. As we continue to abide by His word and follow His guidance, we will keep going from glory to glory until the earth is filled with the full knowledge of the glory of God.

The truth you know about Yahusha is what enables you to live a life of fulfilment. Your understanding of who He is, will help you to become who He has made you to be. There is absolutely no one who has a good relationship with Yahusha that doesn't fulfil purpose; everyone mentioned in the Bible who knew God and walked faithfully with Him, lived a fulfilled life! They all had one goal in common, to draw men to Christ. As children of the Most High God Elohiym! If we do not impart others with the gospel of Adonai and draw sinners to Yahusha Ha-Mashiach, we are still not living a life of fulfilment! Christ laid down His life for us in order to draw us back to our Father God so that we can have an intimate relationship with Him and fulfil our purpose. Likewise, we must lay aside our priorities and make our LORD and Saviour's will our priorities. So, whatever career you are doing, as long as it aligns with God's word, and as long as you are using it to win souls for the kingdom of God, you're fulfilling your purpose. The reason we have eternal life is because of what Yahusha did for us, and he expects us to tell others about Him; the world will continue to remain in darkness until we do what we are called to do-our heavenly Father's business-to become fishers of men!

Colossians 3:1-2 says: If then you were raised with Christ, seek those things which are above, where Christ is, sitting at the right hand of God. Set your mind on the things above, not on the things on the earth.

2 Corinthians 5:9-10: Paul wrote: So, whether we are here in this body or away from this body, our goal is to please Him. For we must all stand before Christ to

be judged. We will each receive whatever we deserve for the good or evil we have done in this earthly body.

Proverbs 11:10 says: "When the righteous thrive, a city rejoices; When the wicked die, there is joyful shouting" (CSB).

Romans 5:17 says: Those who receive grace and the gift of righteousness will reign in life by Jesus Christ.

We do not receive the gift of righteousness, and the gift of eternal life in vain! We should cherish it with the whole of our body, soul, mind and spirit! The reason Christ gave us the gift of eternal life is for us to share the same gift to others; the gift is for a purpose and that purpose is to declare our LORD Yahusha to the entire world; the entire world is in darkness, we cannot close our mouth and pretend as if nothing is happening in our cities, and our nations.

A lot of evil is taking place daily under our eyes, and we are the ones to stop it, and that is why we are the chosen ones to restrain the forces of darkness; and this is how we can be fulfilled! We have the Spirit of Elohiym in us, when we yield to His leadership, He can then restrain the enemies from advancing. The gift of the Holy Spirit in us cannot be dormant, so let us wake up and engage with the Spirit of God that is in us so that we can do incredible things that eyes have not seen, nor ears have heard. Let us not be like the man who received one talent and dug a ground and hid it (Matthew 25:14-30).

1 Peter 4:10-11 says: As each of you has received a gift (a particular spiritual talent, a gracious divine endowment), employ it for one another as (befits) good trustees of God's many-sided grace (faithful stewards of the extremely diverse powers and gifts granted to Christians by unmerited favour). Whoever speaks, (let him do it as one who utters) oracles of God; whoever renders service, (let him do it) as with the strength which God furnishes abundantly, so that in all things God may be glorified through Jesus Christ (Messiah). To Him be glory and dominion forever and ever (through endless ages). Amen (so be it) AMPC.

Isaiah 52:7 says: How beautiful upon the mountains are the feet of him who brings good news, who proclaims peace, who brings glad tidings of good things, who proclaims salvation, who says to Zion, "Your God reigns."

## Willing to follow Him to the end

Matthew 16:24 Jesus speaks: "If anyone desires to come after Me, let him deny himself, and take up his cross, and follow Me."

When Yahusha called His disciples, they all had their various businesses they were doing. Simon Peter, and Andrew his brother, James and John the sons of Zebedee, were professional skilled fishermen

(Matthew 4:18-22). They have been in the fishing business for years, and everyone in that region knew them for that. They thought they were fulfilling their destinies, because they loved what they were doing and were successful in their career. They never knew Elohiym had a far greater plan for them till the day Jesus approached them and asked them to follow Him, which they did immediately not knowing who Jesus Christ actually was.

According to the Scriptures, we know that it wasn't an easy journey for the disciples to leave their businesses that they had established and were doing for years, and to leave their family members to walk with a man who said He would make them become fishers of men. He didn't say to them, "Hey guys! Follow me! I am the Messiah! I will make you all rich!" He only asked them to follow Him and He will make them fishers of men, which they obeyed immediately. Not knowing what the future holds for them, they just followed Yahusha doing the kingdom work joyfully. And at the end they all lived a life of fulfilment, except Judas Iscariot. Many people who started this faith journey have left it behind! They gave up because they didn't get what they were looking for, and as soon as the devil offered them the riches of this world, they turned their back on the one who created them and followed the one who is their enemy, whose intention is to destroy them in the end. Yahusha said in Matthew 22:14, that many are called but few are chosen!

## Peter's revelation

In Matthew 16:13-17, after the disciples had been with Yahusha for a while, Yahusha one day asked His disciples this question, "Who do people say that the Son of Man is?" He didn't ask this question because He wanted to find out what people are actually saying about Him, after all, He knows the heart and mind of all people! The reason He asked the first question "Who do men say that I am?" was for Him to get to the second question which is the most important part of His ministry, so as to reveal Himself to them that He is the Messiah. The disciple then responded by saying, in verse 14, "Some say, you are John the Baptist, some say you're Elijah, or one of the Prophets." And Yahusha then immediately asked the second question, which was the main reason for the first question, "But who do you say that I am?" Simon Peter then answered and said, "You are the Christ, the Son of the living God."

In verse 17, As soon as Peter revealed the true identity of Yahusha, He said immediately to him, "Blessed are you, Simon Bar-Jonah, for flesh and blood has not revealed this to you, but My Father Yahuah who is in heaven."

This revelation of Peter knowing the truth of the Messiah's identity turned everything around for the disciples and for the body of Yahusha. This was the moment Yahusha was waiting for, to reveal Himself to His friends, for them to come to the full knowledge of who He is. Based on the revelation of Peter; Yahusha then affirms that His church will be built on this revelation of Peter, "The rock which is Christ" and He then gave His authority to His church, that whatever His church (Believers) would bind on earth, will be bound in heaven, and whatever His church will loose on earth, will be loosed in heaven (Matthew 16:18-19).

## The unity of the body of Yahusha

Since Elohiym Yahusha is the head of His church, we were brought together from every tribe and tongue to become His body! The only way the body of Christ can be fulfilled is when the whole body of Yahusha agrees to work together in love, in obedience, in honouring one another, strengthening each other, in humility, in godliness, in faith, in kindness, and in patience. Each part of the body has a special unique work to do that would help the other parts grow. The body can only be healthy and produce good fruit when each part of the body works together in unity to help one another!

If the disciples of Yahusha did not work together as one, they wouldn't have been able to fulfil what God had called them to do. The kingdom of God cannot be divided! If it is divided, then it will not stand! The reason the body of Christ has not been able to fulfil its purpose yet, is because of division, lack of revelation of the truth, lack of love, no humility, and greed. And that is why believers are struggling in living a life of obedience and fulfilling their purpose.

1 Corinthians 12:25-27 says: So that there should be no division or discord or lack of adaptation (of the parts of the body to each other), but the members all alike

should have a mutual interest in and care for one another. And if one member suffers, all the parts (share) the suffering; if one member is honoured, all the members share in) the enjoyment of it. Now you (collectively) are Christ's body and (individually) you are members of it, each part severally and distinct (each with his own place and function) AMPC.

Matthew 12:25: Jesus speaks: "Every kingdom divided against itself is brought to desolation, and every city or house divided against itself will not stand.

Ephesians 4:16 says: From whom the whole body, joined and knit together by what every joint supplies, according to the effective working by which every part does its share, causes growth of the body for the edifying of itself in love.

    The reason believers come together is not just to worship the Most High God and go back to their homes, it is for equipping and strengthening each other to grow in their walk with the Holy Spirit and get to the full potential of their destiny. Because if it was only to worship God, everyone can worship God from their homes; but God designed it this way for His children to come together to worship Him as one body and as a family, and to be strengthened and be equipped in the full knowledge of Christ in order to fulfil their purposes.

Ephesians 4:11-13 wrote: Now these are the gifts Christ gave to the church, the apostles, the prophets, the evangelists, and the pastors and teachers. Their responsibility is to equip God's people to do His work and build up the church, the body of Christ. This will continue until we come to such unity in our faith and knowledge of God's Son that we will be mature in the LORD, measuring up to the full and complete standard of Christ (NLT).

Millions of Christians might not be able to live a life of fulfilment because they are under the leadership of ravening wolves; they are like sheep ready to be slaughtered! They are completely lost, and it will be hard for such people to live a life of fulfilment, unless God intervenes. So, this is the time to be wise and have discernment if you don't want to fall prey to these false ministers that are parading everywhere as an angel of light. This is the time to have a personal intimate relationship with Yahusha! We do not have too much time to play around, the Messiah is coming back very soon.

## A new man

In Acts 2, after the Apostles had received the Holy Spirit, they became new men, from fishermen to Apostles of Christ! What a transformation! Although Apostle Paul was not one of the original twelve disciples of Yahusha, he went from being a murderer to becoming one of the greatest Apostles that wrote seven books in the New Testament! What a conversion! On the day of Pentecost, more than three thousand people were saved (Acts 2:41). The Scribes, Pharisees and the religious leaders were all surprised and amazed at their boldness because they knew that these men were uneducated and untrained. These men were radical, they turned the whole nation around, the Pharisees, Scribes and the religious leaders were all frightened because of these men.

Acts 4:13 says: Now when they saw the boldness of Peter and John, and perceived that they were uneducated and untrained men, they marvelled. And they realised that they had been with Jesus.

You have been born again for years, but it is as if you just gave your life to Christ. No changes! Still operating in the same way, you were operating five, ten years ago; my friend, it is time to change! You go to church on Sunday morning and that's it! No time to study the word of God; no time to pray, you are just doing your own thing, and you are claiming that you're in a relationship with God. you have time to go partying, you have time to watch all kinds of tv programmes, you have time to watch football games, politics, documentaries, and the list continues, but you don't have time for God! Someone who is born again will have time to study the word of God, will have time to pray, and will have time to evangelise! So, wake up from your laziness, pull yourself up and start spending time in God's presence.

## Your mindset shapes your destiny

The kingdom of God is a mystery, the creation of humanity is a mystery. So, for you to be able to fulfil God's plans for your life, your mind must be renewed. It is only when your mind has been renewed with the truth, you can be able to do all that God has called you to do and live a life of fulfilment; If you don't know your true identity in Christ, it will be impossible to live a life of fulfilment. The world is waiting for the sons of God Elohiym to manifest His glory! You must see beyond your present situation and see with your faith eyes where God is taking you to.

In Genesis 13:14-15, God told Abraham "Look as far as you can see in every direction-north and south, east and west; I am giving all this land, as far as you can see, to you and your descendants as a permanent possession. (NLT)

Philippians 4:8 says: "Finally, brethren, whatever things are true, whatever things are noble, whatever things are just, whatever things are pure, whatever things are lovely, whatever things are of good report, if there is any virtue and if there is anything praiseworthy-meditate on these things.

2 Corinthians 5 says: Therefore, if anyone is in Christ, he is a new creation; Old things have passed away; Behold! All things have become new.

1 Peter 2:9 says: "But you are a chosen generation, a royal priesthood, a holy nation, His own special people, that you may proclaim the praises of Him who called you out of darkness into His marvellous light;"

The Almighty God has deposited so much in each of everyone of His children! Everything we need is inside of us, because we have the Holy Spirit in us. The only thing that is lacking is your obedience to God's word, acquiring knowledge and revelation to do what He wants you to do so that you can live a life of fulfilment. As a doctor, you have an assignment to do! As a pastor, you have an assignment to do. As a politician, you have an assignment to do! As a gospel artist, you have an assignment to do! As a businessman or woman, you have an assignment to do! Each one of us has a unique assignment to do for the kingdom of God on this earth using our talents.

Your mind must be renewed to know the truth that you are now a new creation in Christ; old things have passed away; behold! All things are now new: we have the life of Christ in us! We belong to a new kingdom with a new King, which is Yahusha Ha-Mashiach! We are God's chosen vessels, special beings, fearfully and wonderfully made. We are set apart from the rest of the world! We are His royal priesthood! Chosen to show forth His magnificence and glory; we are all unique in our own ways! This means we can do all things through the grace and knowledge we have in Christ to bring glory and honour to His Holy name. We were created for a special purpose, specially selected by God to spread His word and bring truth and light to people around the world. This is a special gift from God, so we should use it wisely in serving one another and spreading the gospel of Yahusha Adonai.

John 6:38: Jesus speaks: "For I have come down from heaven, not to do My will, but the will of Him who sent Me."

## Extraordinary life in Christ

Before Elohiym made us, He knew us, and He had predetermined the destiny or the future of everyone (Jeremiah 1:5); if the Apostles of Jesus lived an extraordinary life and did great things in the early church, then we have no excuse not to do great things on this earth to glorify His name before we go back to Him or He returns. God's vision for our lives is greater than what we have experienced so far! It took Him just six days according to Genesis 1, to create the whole world; so, turning our lives around for His glory will cause Him nothing. If people in the world who don't have the Holy Spirit could do great things in this world, don't you think believers that have the Holy Spirit in them are supposed to do greater things through Christ, bringing glory to His name? If we obey His commandments and walk with Him in faith, we will be very surprised how things will change in our lives and in the nations of the earth.

Romans 8:29-30 says: "For whom He foreknew, He also predestined to be conformed to the image of His

Son, that He might be the firstborn among many brethren. Moreover, whom He predestined, these He also called; whom He called, these He also justified, and whom He justified, these He also glorified."

John 14:12: Jesus speaks: "Most assuredly, I say to you, he who believes in Me, the works that I do he will do also; and greater works than these he will do, because I go to My Father."

The will of Yahusha Adonai is for us to abide in Him. It is when we abide in Him that we can become fruitful and live a life of fulfilment. We cannot do it on our own! We all need our Father God who made us and put us in our mother's womb, to lead and guide us on the right path to fulfil our assignments that would bring honour and glory to His Holy name which is the reason for our existence. Whatever thing we are doing in this kingdom, has to bring glory to God!

Those that are led by the Spirit of God are the true sons of God! We walk by faith and not by what we see or feel. Abraham left his father's house to an unknown land when Elohiym asked him to leave! He obeyed and followed God's instruction till the end. And Elohiym the Most High God not only blessed him but also his descendants. Abraham became God's best friend (Genesis 12). You can only live a life of fulfilment when you follow His will and plans for your life!

Hebrews 11:8 says: "By faith Abraham obeyed when he was called to go out to the place which he would receive as an inheritance. And he went out, not knowing where he was going." (NKJV)

## Unholy lifestyle can stop us from fulfilling our destiny

Living in an unholy way stops us from fulfilling the plans of God for our lives! It is like a deadly virus that destroys our whole being. God has laid down His laws for us to abide by; every sin we commit has its consequences. The Scripture says in Romans 6:23: "For the wages of sin is death." Many afflictions that have held people bound are due to sin; most times demons afflict people with illnesses when there is sin at work. Someone that is living in sin is still a slave to the devil, which is why demonic beings will make sure people are living a lifestyle of immorality that will separate them from the presence of Elohiym.

I am not saying that every sickness is due to sin, No! After all, so many men and women who lived for God got sick and died. Since Satan feeds on the flesh, we should try to avoid it by living holy. We should honour and respect the Spirit of God that is in us because our body is His temple, if we are truly born again. The kingdom of God is for the true sons and daughters of God, those who do not grieve the Holy Spirit by living a life of immorality.

1 Corinthians 3:16 says: Do you not know that you are the temple of God and that the Spirit of God dwells in you.

John 8:34-35: Jesus said: "Most assuredly, I say to you, whoever commits sin is a slave of sin. And a slave does not abide in the house forever, but a son abides forever.

Many believers are going from church to church looking for miracles when the miracle is just for them to repent and seek God diligently. Do not let immorality stop you from fulfilling the plans and purpose of God for your life. Because of disobedience, Adam and Eve lost their purpose and brought curse on themselves and to all humans till Christ came and died for the whole world, and whoever believes in Him shall be saved. So, anything that you are doing that is contrary to God's commandments, repent and give your life to Christ before it is too late! Seek Him diligently! He will surely show up in your life and turn things around for good.

Proverbs 28:13 says: Whoever conceals their sins does not prosper, but the one who confesses and renounces them finds mercy (NIV).

Proverbs 14:12 says: "There is a way that seems right to a person, but its end is the way to death." (CSB)

My fellow brothers and sisters, it is time to arise from whatever has been holding you down from living a life of fulfilment! It is time to shine out the light that is inside of you. It is time to break free from all demonic forces that have made you live a life of mediocrity! Be set free from every addiction that has kept you in darkness preventing you from living a life that is pleasing to God; you are created to operate on this earth as king and priest, to live a life of fulfilment, you are not a slave to sin, you are a child of the Creator of the universe.

Isaiah 60:1 says: Arise, shine; For your light has come! And the glory of the LORD God is risen upon you.

Isaiah 52:1-3 says: Awake, awake! Put on your strength, o Zion; Put on your beautiful garments, o Jerusalem, the holy city! For the uncircumcised and the unclean shall no longer come to you. Shake yourself from the dust, arise; Sit down, o Jerusalem! Loose yourself from the bonds of your neck, o captive daughter of Zion! For thus says the LORD God Almighty: "You have sold yourselves for nothing, and you shall be redeemed without money."

## Your destiny is written in a book

Everyone's destiny is written in God's book in heaven; before we were formed in our mother's womb, God had already written down His plans for us (Jeremiah 29:11). So, the question is, how do we know His plans for our life and how do we fulfil it? It is only through the Holy Spirit who knows all things, He will reveal it to us and help us to fulfil whatever is written of us in His book. No one would be able to accomplish the things God Almighty has written down for our lives without our total obedience to His laws; it is like a student who never studied nor took instructions from their teacher, do you think that student will pass his exam and move to the next class? Likewise, the Holy Spirit is our Tutor. The reason He is here on earth is to train and guide us so that we would become exactly what is written of us. But if we fail to follow His instruction, then we are giving the devil and his cohorts an open invitation into our lives.

Psalm 139:16 says: Your eyes watched me before I was born. Before I had seen the light of day, you decided how many days I would live! You wrote it down in your book.

It is never too late to start again, to fulfil that dream God laid in your heart all these years. I never knew God Almighty had a greater plan for me all these years till I surrendered my life totally to Him, so that He can use it for His glory. You have so much in you that only the Spirit of God can bring out. Until we pour ourselves a drink offering unto our God, it will be hard for us to accomplish all that is written of us in God's book in heaven. "God is not looking for a self-righteous person to use! He is seeking to use those that have made themselves available, willing to carry their cross and follow Him, those that are humble." So, keep fighting the good fight of faith till you return back to Him.

2 Timothy 4:7-8, Apostle Paul speaks: I have fought the good fight, I have finished the race, I have kept the faith. Finally, there is laid up for me the crown of

righteousness, which the LORD God, the righteous Judge, will give to me on that day, and not to me only but also to all who have loved His appearing.

May Elohiym bless you and grant you the grace to strive to do greater and extraordinary things on this earth that would bring glory and honour to His Holy name; refuse to settle for anything lesser than the plans and purpose of God for your life. The ruler of this world has been defeated by our LORD and Saviour Yahusha Ha-Mashiach; so, yield to the Spirit of God and He will grant you the grace to live a life of fulfilment. You are made for signs and wonders, you are a king and a priest here on this earth to manifest God in every aspect of your life, because He lives in you, and He is with you
Shalom!

# Chapter Ten

# EXCEEDING JOY

Many people see obedience to Adonai's commandments as a burden, but actually it is the doorway to overflowing joy and fulfillment in life. We are living in a world that often equates freedom with doing whatever we please, Jesus Christ words teaches us a higher truth—real freedom and lasting joy are only found in living according to His ways.

Jesus Christ said in John 15:10-11: " As the Father loved Me, I also have loved you; abide in My love. If you keep My commandments, you will abide in My love, just as I have kept My Father's commandments and abide in His love. These things I have spoken to you, that My joy may remain in you, and that your joy may be full.

The joy Jesus offers is not temporary or shallow! It is complete, overflowing, and deeply rooted in our relationship with Him. When we obey Adonai's commandments, we align our hearts with His! We live with purpose, clarity, and peace. Even in trials, our obedience anchors us in hope and produces a joy that the world cannot steal!

Let us not see Elohiym's commands as restrictions, but as invitations to walk closely with Him; every act of obedience draws us nearer to the heart of Adonai—and in His presence, there is fullness of joy (Psalms 16:11).

So, choose obedience; not out of duty, but out of love! And in doing so, you will step into a joy that is exceeding, abundant, and eternal!

Psalms 119:1-2 says: Joyful are people of integrity, who follow the instructions of the LORD. Joyful are those who obey His laws and search for Him with all their hearts (NLT).

As Believers we are not moved by any kind of circumstances, but by the words of Jesus; we rejoice regardless of what our circumstances are. Our joy does not come from the world, wealth, or from people but only from Adonai! When we surrender to His will, that is when we will have overflowing Joy and peace that surpasses every human understanding. True joy is a result of the Holy Spirit working in us (Galatians 5:22), when we obey God's commands, we are walking in the Spirit, and joy follows naturally! And this is what the Apostles experienced during their time on earth; they were filled with the Holy Spirit and hence their lives were filled with overflowing joy; even when they went through persecutions cf (Acts 13:49-52); (Acts 17:41), they count it all joy for being worthy of Christ; they were still filled with joy; knowing they would share Christ's glory.

1 Peter 4:13 says: But rejoice to the extent that you partake of Christ's sufferings, that when His glory is revealed, you may also be glad with exceeding joy.

Psalms 43:4 says: Then will I go unto the altar of Elohiym, unto El my exceeding joy: yea, upon the harp will I praise you, O Elohiym Elohai (CEPHER).

    Here, the psalmist called Adonai his "exceeding joy" — the source of our greatest joy and happiness should come from the Almighty God Adonai, by completely putting our trust in Him. Exceeding joy is a deep, overwhelming happiness and peace that goes beyond normal happiness–it is an intense, divine spiritual joy that comes from the Almighty God's presence, His promises, and His works. Exceeding joy is often connected with God's salvation, His deliverance, and overwhelming goodness, His favor, fulfilling of God's promises; it is anchored from Adonai's character and His faithfulness!

Jude 1:24 says: "Now to Him who is able to keep you from stumbling, and to present you blameless before the presence of His glory with exceeding joy."

    Therefore it doesn't matter what our present circumstances are, we should keep on rejoicing even in suffering and be exceedingly glad because of the coming glory. Each time we obey the instructions of Elohiym, and keep rejoicing, there's a shift in the spirit realm; things begin to happen in our favour! In the book of Matthew 2: When the wise men saw the star of the Messiah when He was born, the KING of kings and the LORD of lords, they rejoiced with exceeding great joy knowing that salvation has come to the whole world, and immediately they obeyed and followed the star till they got to the house where our Messiah was born and they worshiped Him! God's ultimate plan is for all His children to have exceeding joy.

Matthew 2:10 says: (The wise men) "When they saw the star, they rejoiced with exceeding great joy."

## The resurrection of the Messiah

Luke 24:1-53: After Jesus was crucified, His Apostles were all terrified and confused, fear of what might happened to them, all their hope was lost; When Jesus Christ had risen and the women not knowing that He was risen, went to His tomb in order to anoint His body, as a customary practice to honour the dead in Jewish tradition, intending to complete the final rites of burial; they then found out that the tomb was opened and Jesus was not there, so they were greatly perplexed about it. And when the two angels appeared to them and told them that He was risen and reminded them of His words in Verse 6-7; they returned and informed the rest of the eleven Apostles of Jesus Christ, but they did not believe them.

Then Verse 13, Two of Jesus followers were on their way to a villages called Emmaus, they were sad and filled with grief, and were arguing and discouraged; Jesus appeared to them and asked the matter, why they were sad and they told Jesus the sad news of His death and how they were hoping Jesus will be the one to redeem Israel. Then in Verse 25-26, Jesus said to them how foolish and unbelieve they are to all the prophecies of the prophets:

Unbelieve is what often stops us from having exceeding joy as children of Adonai. If we put our faith in His words and things happen contrary to our expectation, we should always be assured that His words are forever settled concerning our lives and so we rejoice exceedingly because we walk by faith and not by sight!

So when the men got to where they were going, they urged Jesus to spend the night with them which Jesus accepted! And while they were on the table, Jesus took the bread, blessed and broke it and gave it to them. And as soon as they ate it their eyes were opened and they knew Him, and immediately Jesus disappeared from their sight. They immediately forgot all their sorrow and were exceedingly rejoicing and went straight to Jerusalem to tell the rest of the disciples the good news that our LORD Jesus Christ had truly been raised from the dead and had appeared to them.

And as the Apostles were still trying to grasp the whole story; Jesus appeared and stood by them and said to them in Verse 36, "Peace to you!" They became terrified thinking they had seen a ghost; and this is what happened to most of us, when Adonai speaks to us through His words, or through dreams, or even through someone, specially if what He is revealing to us is huge; we starts getting terrified and allow doubt to come, hence causing delay to our breakthrough and joy!

Luke 38-39 Jesus speaks: "Why are you troubled?" He asked them. "And why do doubts arise in your hearts? Look at my hands and my feet, that it is I Myself! Touch Me and see, because a ghost does not have flesh and bones as you can see I have."

And as soon as Jesus spoke these words, He showed them His hands and feets, He then asked if they had anything to eat so as to prove to them He is truly alive and not a ghost.

And in Verse 46-47, He went further to explain the Scriptures to them and their understanding were opened; He then blessed them and while He was still blessing them, He was taken up to Heaven. As the Apostles finished worshipping Him, they returned to Jerusalem with exceedingly great joy!

The fact that we are children of the Most High God Adonai should make us rejoice exceedingly! That is why it is very important for us to walk with Him in obedience always because this is the path to true freedom in Christ!

Philippians 4:4 says: Rejoice in Yahweh always: and again I say, Rejoice. (CEPHER)

## Hannah's Joy

In 1 Samuel 1:1-28: It was recorded how Hannah was barren for many years and suffered deep sorrow; But she never gave up her hope and faith in Yahuah that He will one day remember her and so He did; Yahua remembered her and gave her a child and he was name Samuel! She was overwhelmed with exceeding joy and burst into prayer!

## Hannah's Prayer

"My heart rejoices in the LORD; My horn is exalted in the LORD. I smile at my enemies, Because I rejoice in Your Salvation (1 Samuel 2:1) NKJV.

## Key Point
1. Hannah's barren womb was opened- impossible in human eyes; causing overwhelming joy
2. Hannah's prayer praises Adonai's power, justice, and faithfulness.
3. Hannah fulfilled her vow by given Samuel back to Adonai
4. Samuel became a priest in the house of Adonai, serving Adonai with integrity

## The chosen ones

1 Peter 2:9 says: "But you are a chosen people, a royal priesthood, a holy nation, God's special possession, that you may declare the praises of Him who called you out of darkness into His wonderful light."

Apostle Peter wrote this letter to the early christians when they were scattered across Asia Minor and facing persecution and alienation for their faith; Amidst their suffering, Peter offers both encouragement and a powerful reminder of their identity in Christ; this Scripture encapsulates both the calling and the mission of the Christian believer.

Deuteronomy 7:6 says: "For you are a holy people to the LORD your God; the LORD your God has chosen you to be a people for Himself, a special treasure above all the peoples on the face of the earth (NKJV).

Peter first affirms the believer's new identity by using rich Old Testament language! This phrase echoes God's description of Israel in (Deuteronomy 7:6:). Thereby, Peter is not erasing Israel's role but rather extending God's covenantal word to include all believers in Christ, both Jew and Gentile!

This identity is not based on nationality or merit, but on Yahweh's Sovereign choice and grace!

The phrase "a royal priesthood" suggests a dual role; believers are both royalty and priests! As royalty, they share in Christ's reign, as priests, they are called to mediate Adonai's presence to the world through worship, prayer, and holy living. In the Old Testament, only a selected group could serve as priests, but now every believer has direct access to Father God Yahuah through Christ!

Calling the church a "holy nation" signifies a collective identity set apart for Elohiym's purposes. Holiness is not merely moral purity, but separation from the world's values to belong to Jesus Christ! This echoes the idea that Christians are sojourners, citizens of a Heavenly Kingdom.

Finally, "God's special possession" underscores the deep value and intimacy of Adonai's relationship with His people; that we belong to Him not as slaves, but as beloved sons and daughters. This belonging carries a purpose: "that you may declare the praises of Him who called you out of darkness into His wonderful light." The identity of the believer is not an end in itself, but a calling to worship and witness! We are to proclaim the goodness and glory of Adonai, who delivered us from spiritual darkness into the light of truth, love, and eternal life; this is our true joy!

John 3:16 says: "For God so loved the world, that He gave His only begotten Son, that whoever believes in Him should not perish but have eternal life."

Revelation 22:5 says: "And there will no longer be night; they have no need for lamplight or sunlight, because the LORD God will illumine them; and they will reign as kings forever and ever (AMP)

We are living in a world where identity is often based on social status, race, nationality, or success, 1 Peter 2:9 offers a radically different foundation: identity rooted in Jesus Christ love, grace and calling! It is both a comfort and a challenge—a comfort in the sense that believers are deeply known and valued by Adonai, and a challenge because they are called to live in a way that reflects that identity!

In conclusion, 1 Peter 2:9 is a cornerstone verse for understanding the dignity, responsibility, and mission of the Christian community! It reminds believers that they are not forgotten or abandoned, when going through trials and persecutions, but chosen and commissioned. In the face of suffering or marginalization; this verse lifts the hearts of the faithful ones and redirects their focus to their true calling; to live as Yahweh's children and proclaim His light to this dying world.

Psalms 21:6-7 says: " For you have made him most blessed forever; You have made him exceedingly glad with Your presence. For the King trusts in the LORD, and through the mercy of the Most High he shall not be moved." NKJV

## Prayer

Dear Heavenly Father, thank you for the gift of Salvation that brought exceeding joy and strength to us; Grant us the grace to always walk in faith and remain in your presence that our joy will be overflowing always regardless of what we might be going through in life, knowing that you are more than able to bring us out from our problems and challenges.
May you grant us the boldness to continually praise you and share the amazing gift of Salvation to those

around us, in the mighty name of our LORD and Saviour Jesus Christ Amen.

# REFERENCES

## Bible Versions

- Amplified Bible
- Amplified Bible, Classic Edition
- Christian Standard Bible
- Easy English Bible 2024
- English Standard Version 2016
- King James Version
- Legacy Standard Bible
- New International Version
- Cepher @2024 Publishing Group
- New King James Version
- New Living Translation
- The Message Version
- World Messianic Bible

## Books

- Graham, Billy. *Peace with God: The Secret of Happiness.*
- Graham, Billy. *What Happened at the Cross.*
- Graham, Billy. *The Holy Spirit: Activating God's Power in Your Life.*

- Graham, Billy. *Living by Faith in an Uncertain World.*
- Graham, Billy. *Nearing Home: Life, Faith, and Finishing Well.*
- Warren, Rick. *The Purpose Driven Life.*

## Additional Resources

- Google Search

www.ingramcontent.com/pod-product-compliance
Lightning Source LLC
Chambersburg PA
CBHW040245010526
44119CB00057B/817